The ▲ Abrams Guide to American House Styles

BY **WILLIAM MORGAN** PHOTOGRAPHY BY **RADEK KURZAJ**

DRAWINGS AND GLOSSARY BY **NED PRATT** EDITED BY **RICHARD OLSEN**

HARRY N. ABRAMS, INC., PUBLISHERS

contents

DESIGNER: Brankica Kovrlija
PRODUCTION MANAGER: Maria Pia Gramaglia
COPYEDITING: Richard G. Gallin
EDITORAL ASSISTANCE: Josh Faught, Sigi Nacson

LIBRARY OF CONGRESS CATALOGING-IN-PUBLICATION DATA

Morgan, William, 1944–
The Abrams guide to American house styles / by William Morgan ;
photography by Radek Kurzaj ; drawings and glossary by Ned Pratt ;
edited by Richard Olsen.
p. cm.
Includes bibliographical references and index.
ISBN 0-8109-4943-1
1. Architecture, Domestic—United States. I. Title.

NA7205.M6793 2004
728'.37'0973—dc22

2004000111

PRINTED AND BOUND IN CHINA
10 9 8 7 6 5 4 3 2 1

HARRY N. ABRAMS, INC.
100 Fifth Avenue
New York, NY 10011
www.abramsbooks.com

Abrams is a subsidiary of

LA MARTINIÈRE

acknowledgments

The Abrams Guide to American House Styles is a collaborative effort. Although the responsibility for errors in fact and judgment is mostly mine, the book's contents are the result of years of study and teaching—and learning from my students.

Much of what I was taught about American houses by Professors Hugh Morrison, James Marston Fitch, and especially George Tatum (at Dartmouth, Columbia, and Delaware, respectively) is echoed here. Over the years the schools at which I have taught have supported research and travel. In addition to Princeton University, the University of Louisville, and Roger Williams University, a number of organizations have underwritten my work, including the National Endowment for the Humanities, the American Friends of Attingham, and the Smithsonian Institution.

Ned Pratt not only enlivened the text with his drawings, he wrote the Glossary and served as an invaluable research assistant. Radek Kurzaj indomitably crisscrossed America to take the images that are the heart of the book. This is my second project for Abrams under the inspired direction of Richard Olsen.

Most of all, I have been blessed with a restored 1915 Georgian Revival house in which to write. My wife Carolyn not only renovated the house, she contributed immeasurably to this book. — WILLIAM MORGAN

The editor extends thanks to the many who made it possible for us to locate and photograph the houses featured in this book. Special thanks go to Diane Maddex of Archetype Press, Bruce Brooks Pfeiffer of the Frank Lloyd Wright Foundation; Beth Morton of the Eufala Heritage Association; Ken Horton of the Roebuck Springs Historical Preservation Society; Lynda Page of the Lower Cape Fear Historical Society; Jay Pridmore of Chicago; Kris and Larry Olsen of Phoenix; Diane Garbutt of Houston; Dan and Elizabeth Garbutt of Dallas; Michael Webb of Los Angeles; Randy Nauert of Malibu; Stephen Fox of Rice University; Catherine Bishir of the University of North Carolina; Thomas Barrie of North Carolina State University; Robert Russell of The College of Charleston; and to the work of Robert Winter and the late David Gebhard.

about the photographs

Each of the featured houses was photographed from public property using either a perspective-correcting lens or one of a variety of telephoto lenses.

editor's preface

IN THIS THE FIRST EDITION OF *The Abrams Guide to American House Styles* we have tried to simplify—in text, image, and graphic presentation—what has become a complex subject to understand, resulting in a book that, we hope, will easily be used by many for years to come. We have tried to make it compact enough to be of use both at the desk and out in the neighborhood. It is the first book of its scope to be produced all in color, a feature that will undoubtedly make it among the most accessible of its genre. What distinguishes one architectural style from the next can in some instances be quite subtle, reduced to little more than the stylistic appointments adorning a house's front entranceway. Seeing the examples of each style up-close and in new color photography, as we have provided here, is a benefit we think readers will appreciate. ■ Then there are also the often complicated regional variations of each style to contend with: the Colonial Revival in Spring Lake, New Jersey, for instance, can appear quite different from the Colonial Revival in River Oaks in Houston, Texas, or in San Marino, California. There are other complexities, of course. For instance, is it true that a Queen Anne–style house should never be painted white if it is to be historically accurate? Is a Modern-style house "modern" today? We have tried to address such concerns and more; whenever possible we photographed examples of each style as it can be found region to region across the continental United States and have included with each photograph the location city and recognized date of construction. There are 23 styles, nearly 400 houses in all, presented in the book. ■ In crisscrossing the United States multiple times in the past three years to compile this volume, we found that Americans remain very attuned to matters of style when it comes to their homes. There are those styles that dominate no matter the region, such as the Colonial Revival and the Victorian-era styles. Despite the counter-efforts of those including our greatest architect of houses, Frank Lloyd Wright, Americans continue to love their English Victorian styles, no question about it. ▪ Arguably, all but two of the styles shown in this book originated outside the United States, and in our travels across the country we encountered multiple new-construction examples of nearly every one of them. Which begs one to ask, are homebuyers at all concerned with whether their house is a truly American style of architecture, as Wright sought to create and popularize nearly a century ago? Wright would be pleased to see that one of his proposed solutions to this quandary, the Prairie Style, is gaining in favor once again. The Ranch House, a house type that has evolved into a style and is the other that we can call ours, is also in the midst of rediscovery. Neither of these styles, though, is likely to regain the aesthetic hold they had on parts of the country during their boom years, the early twentieth and mid-twentieth century, respectively. If one factors in the stylistically ambiguous mass-produced builder-developer houses of today, hope for a widely accepted American style of house might appear to be fast slipping away. After all, it is these houses that represent the majority of new construction. Have the builder-developers, through their seemingly haphazard merging of features taken from a plethora of historical styles (most are borrowed from England, France, and Spain) created a uniquely American style of house by accident? Given the rich diversity of the country's population, such a blending would be very much in character, very American. ▪ The majority of the examples shown in *The Abrams Guide* are architect-designed houses, many of which were designed by some of the United States's most revered architects: Alexander Jackson Davis, McKim, Mead & White, Julia Morgan, Frank Lloyd Wright, Greene & Greene, David Adler, Irving Gill, Wallace Neff, Harwell Harris, Louis Kahn, and Frank Gehry. Many of these houses could be characterized as iconic, if not pure, examples of their respective style. For those seeking a new house in a particular historical style, or preparing for a historically accurate restoration of an older home, scores of the examples showcased in the book would be appropriate models for stylistic emulation.

introduction

ARCHITECTURE is one of the ways we give meaning to who we are. We invent styles to help us make sense of all the different architectural designs. A style is a label, a grouping of characteristics that allows us to identify salient aspects of our history. In domestic architecture, style is a way of defining the houses we have built; style expresses our worldview, our aspirations. ▪ What we build is as revealing as the stories we write or the legislation we pass. But of the physical presence of who we are, nothing is as important as our houses—that most basic of units of human settlement. Our houses *are* us, and this is especially true in America, a land of immigrants who came here in large part to follow the dream of individual home ownership. A person's home is the yardstick of success in this country, and style defines the houses that define the people who build them or choose to live in them. Style, then, is both a useful tool in describing houses and a manifestation of deeper meaning. ▪ Do we need another guidebook to American houses? *The Abrams Guide to American House Styles* is not intended to replace the many guides that we have relied upon for years, sometimes decades. But a lot has happened since the pioneering regional studies of the early twentieth century and the more sophisticated volumes of late spawned by a growing cadre of professionally trained historians and preservationists. We know much more now than we did when I enrolled in *Art I: Introduction to Architecture* in 1963. Yet, at times it seems as though greater historical accuracy has come at the price of clarity. ■ Our goal here is a readable and richly illustrated introduction to the styles—for everyone, from homeowner to architect. *The Abrams Guide* is meant to augment those many writers on architecture upon whose shoulders we are standing. ■ It does seem, though, that the proliferation of styles and stylistic names can be a bit overwhelming. Current building styles rarely seem to last more than a decade, and even then the law of simultaneity assures no simple demarcation between a past or present style. ■ Also, past styles used to be *past*. But now every suburban developer seems to be reaching into our nation's architectural attic—not necessarily for inspiration, but for details. The revived style-of-the-month hardly pays suitable homage to its source. Like fashions to be recycled at whim, styles seem to have become all the same, so that value judgments become less meaningful. ■ A certain confusion results from the indiscriminate borrowing from the past. Does adding a Palladian window to a balloon-frame house covered in polyvinyl siding make it a Georgian house? Does mixing several styles in a single house cloud the lessons the past style might have to teach us?   Still, it is worthwhile—even our responsibility—to attempt to re-assess America's past and our house styles. Further understanding of who we are and why we choose to build as we do may help us make smarter decisions about how we build for the future.

01

colonial

THERE COULD HARDLY BE A MORE EVOCATIVE WORD attached to the American house than *Colonial*. For most people, it implies a simpler and happier, morally upright time: *Colonial* suggests Early American, what some view as a golden age of George Washington and Benjamin Franklin, bucolic farms and small villages peopled by noble settlers striving to create our unique national values. Connotations of servitude to a foreign power seem to have been swept to the background by positive associations of an Edenic era before railroads, factories, and urban sprawl. Label any product, service, or location "Colonial," and it takes on a patriotic aura.

It seems unlikely that we Americans will never abandon such a beloved and ingrained term. Nonetheless, Colonial can serve a useful purpose if closely defined. We will use it to identify the houses of the early European settlement period, primarily the seventeenth century.

Very few houses erected before 1700 survive, and many of those are restorations of varying degrees of authenticity. Early homes were updated or replaced, burned, abandoned, or fell into ruin. The physical and written record, however, gives us a good picture of our first houses, and these were, for the most part, re-creations of the homes that the early settlers knew back home. Englishmen built English cottages, the Dutch erected houses in Nieuw Amsterdam that looked like those they left behind in Holland, while Spanish and French colonists recalled the building methods and materials of their native lands when they built houses in California and the Mississippi River Valley.

A yeoman from East Anglia who was familiar with timber framing used it to construct a house in Massachusetts, even though his fields were full of stone. After a winter or two, he realized that thatched roofs and exposed half-timber walls were less than ideal, although the environmentally dictated changes did not alter the steep pitch of the roof, originally developed for narrow English streets. Small windows were less a function of defense against Native American raiders than a traditional form shaped by the rarity and high cost of glass.

The Dutch settlers in New Jersey and New York felt most comfortable with the ubiquitous brick of the Netherlands; the characteristic stepped gables are remembrances of the Old World, rather than Americanisms. The broad protecting porches built by the French settlers may have made more sense in Louisiana than along the St. Lawrence River, but the form was as cultural as practical. One import that achieved tremendous lasting power was the log house, brought from northern Europe to the shores of the Delaware by Swedes and Finns. The adaptability of the log cabin made it a favorite with all immigrant groups as they moved westward over the Appalachians from the middle of the eighteenth century on, and it became a national icon.

But the Cape Cod cottage was the seventeenth-century type that survived and evolved as one of the most popular, thoroughly American styles. The Cape developed from the earliest English cottages—a humble, rural dwelling, low on the ground, built around a central chimney, and constructed with lots of sheltering roof. This Colonial type never went out of fashion, although it was constantly modified, and it is found from coast to coast as the ideal starter home, an economical, imminently sensible reflection of the idea of home.

HALSEY HOUSE, **1648**, Southampton, New York. / **OPPOSITE, TOP: JARVIS-FLEET HOUSE**, **ca. 1653**, Huntington, New York. Bell-shaped gambrel roof shows builder's Dutch origins. / **BOTTOM: JACKSON HOUSE**, **1664**, Portsmouth, New Hampshire. Oldest house in New Hampshire recalls Medieval England.

TOP: **PIETER CLAESE WYCKOFF HOUSE**, **ca. 1652**, Brooklyn, New York. / **BOTTOM: HOUSE**, **ca. 1677**, Lynn-field, Massachusetts. / **OPPOSITE: HOUSE**, **ca. 1660**, Sandwich, Massachusetts. Three-quarter Cape with clapboard front, shingled sides. Sandwich is the oldest town on Cape Cod.

CONFERENCE HOUSE, ca. 1680, Staten Island, New York. Substantial Dutch building with Georgian windows.

MULFORD HOUSE, ca. 1680, East Hampton, New York.

SHELDON HOUSE, ca. 1698, Deerfield, Massachusetts. Projecting upper story; house was burned by Indians in 1704 and reconstructed in the early twentieth century.

FRARY HOUSE, ca. 1689, Deerfield, Massachusetts. Note saltbox shape; large windows are later.

VOORLEZER HOUSE, ca. 1695, Staten Island, New York.

DRAWING: **LUYKAS VAN ALEN HOUSE, 1737**, Kinderhook, New York. / **JABEZ WILDER HOUSE, ca. 1699**, Hingham, Massachusetts. Best known (and maybe the earliest) "bow" house.

OPPOSITE, TOP: HOUSE, ca. 1700, Swansea, Massachusetts. / **BOTTOM: MISS AMELIA'S COTTAGE, ca. 1725**, Amagansett, New York. / **GUYON-LAKE-TYSEN HOUSE, ca. 1740**, Staten Island, New York. Dutch Colonial with characteristic bell-shaped gambrel roof, forming a covered porch.

OPPOSITE: **NATHAN WADE HOUSE, ca. 1751**, Glocester, Rhode Island. / **TOP: ANIEL SMITH HOUSE, ca. 1750**, Providence, Rhode Island. / **BOTTOM: HOUSE, 1754**, Damariscotta, Maine. Settlers from Massachusetts brought Cape Cod cottages to Maine.

TOP: HOUSE, ca. 1790, Dennis, Massachusetts. Traditional Cape Cod with more sophisticated fenestration and doorway treatment. / **BOTTOM: HOUSE, ca. 1800**, Yarmouth, Massachusetts. Classic full Cape along Old King's Highway.

OPPOSITE, TOP: **STEPHAN WINE HOUSE**, **1828**, Sandwich, Massachusetts. Later version of a bow roof Cape. / **BOTTOM: HOUSE**, **ca. 1850**, Sandwich, Massachusetts. Eminently serviceable Cape saltbox gets Greek Revival facade. / **GAMBREL HOUSE**, **ca. 1810**, Deerfield, Massachusetts.

colonial notes on the defining characteristics

GENERAL PROPORTIONS

Tall, narrow.

SPATIAL DESIGNATION AND FLOOR PLAN

Primarily single-story, though examples with overhanging upper stories exist, mostly in New England. One or two bedrooms and almost never two-rooms deep, except in additions, leading to classic saltbox shape (again, mostly in New England).

ROOF TYPES AND FEATURES

Steeply pitched. Double pitched on Dutch and Swedish examples. Dormers present occasionally, especially on examples in the South.

CHIMNEY PLACEMENT

Central chimney in New England; end chimneys in the South.

FENESTRATION

Small windows with tiny panes.

ENTRANCEWAY

Narrow, windowless wooden doors.

STRUCTURAL AND FACEWORK MATERIALS

Mostly timber framing with overlapping clapboards; some brick in the Middle Colonies and the South; some stone in German, Dutch, and Swedish areas.

COLOR

Wooden houses painted earth tones—ochre, red, browns, often vivid but never white. Most Colonial houses, especially rural ones, were not painted at all.

PARSON CAPEN HOUSE, **1683**, Topsfield, Massachusetts.

02

georgian

early georgian

middle georgian

late georgian

GEORGIAN: AN OVERVIEW

Georgian sounds like a more elegant term than *Colonial,* and the architecture of the eighteenth century is indeed more sophisticated, often elegant. The architecture of the mother country finally absorbed the classicism of the ancient world (filtered through the Italian Renaissance) and inspired the architecture of early America. Whereas the cottages of the early settlement period reflected Elizabethan traditions with their tall, asymmetrical forms lit by small windows, Georgian houses were based upon more abstract concepts of design like geometry and proportion. They also had much larger windows—a feature that may echo the humanistic search for clarity but that also reflects changing technology, as glass got bigger, cheaper, and more practical.

With Georgian, we adopt the English convention of identifying a stylistic label with the name of the ruling monarch. Thus, Georgian covers most of the eighteenth century, beginning with the accession of George I (r. 1714–27); George III, the king who lost the American colonies, did not die until 1820, and his son George IV ruled for another decade. Classical architecture had arrived earlier than the Georges, but it had coexisted somewhat uneasily with medieval traditions.

Inigo Jones (1573–1652), the English playwright, stage designer, and architect to King Charles I, had traveled to Italy, and he almost single-handedly introduced classical architecture to England; his Queen's House (begun in 1616 and completed in 1635) at Greenwich, England, became a beachhead for classicism. In shepherding an austere, proportionally correct style based upon the monuments of the past, Jones also spread the influence of the stupendously influential architect Andrea Palladio (1508–1580). The Venetian master's theoretical yet practical treatise *I quattro libri dell'architettura* (*The Four Books of Architecture*) of 1570 became the template for many an English house (eponymously called Neo-Palladian) and eventually many American ones. Palladianism is one of the enduring hallmarks of Georgian.

Georgian contains not only Palladian elements but owes much to the British architects Sir Christopher Wren (1632–1723) and James Gibbs (1674–1754), the first

British architect to be trained in Rome. Gibbs's own book of 1728, *A Book of Architecture* (which borrowed heavily from Palladio), proved enormously influential in spreading Palladianism to Britain's American colonies.

Yet, like the term *Colonial, Georgian* is rather broad. Architecturally, Georgian can be divided into three distinct periods: Early Georgian, Middle Georgian, and Late Georgian. This is not as complicated as it may at first seem, for these are logical and helpful divisions that allow us to more fully understand eighteenth-century house design.

EARLY GEORGIAN

Early Georgian, which dates from the first half of the eighteenth century, did not happen overnight. But the earliest houses of the style demonstrate immediate changes, most noticeable being the desire for symmetry. Georgian is an architecture of appearances; in keeping with its Renaissance legacy, the facade, or public face of a house, was paramount.

Windows are not only larger, but they were double hung (that is, with sashes, not casements), and their placement was carefully considered. As the century progressed, the proportional relationship of the windows to mass and to each other became quite sophisticated. Glass was always expensive, but one can follow the development of Georgian by observing the multipane configurations: as glass got cheaper and better, twelve panes over twelve became a less-favored configuration than larger nine-over-six windows, which were eventually superseded by six over six.

The rooms behind the windows were not always as symmetrical in layout as the fenestration implied, but that was of little consequence, just as the sides and back of a house might not be regular. This even extended to the use of materials, wherein a cheaper material like shingling was employed on the sides of a wood house, while the front had clapboards; on a brick house, the fanciest brick bonding might have been limited to just the front.

Early Georgian houses were not as tall as their predecessors (and throughout the century, the roof continued to evolve to a lower and lower profile), and the new houses appeared more often than not to be square. The sense of height was also diminished by placing the houses upon a basement—or at least a formal platform or plinth, whereas the earlier houses sat right upon the ground. Mentally remove the English roof and one can visualize an Italian Renaissance palazzo. The Georgian house was invariably two rooms deep. This double-pile plan consisted of two rooms situated one behind the other on each side of a central hallway—a form that has remained almost a constant in Georgian and Georgian Revival houses.

Georgian was a universal style along the Atlantic seaboard, although there are noticeable regional differences. The double-pile plan might have its chimneys on the inside walls in New England and on the outside walls in Virginia and Maryland. Also, the New England housebuilders still favored wood; stone and brick predominate in the Middle Colonies; and brick is more associated with the South (there were a lot of wood houses in the South, but they were less likely to survive). Only the most knowledgeable building historian can determine whether a mason in New York or Philadelphia came from an English, Dutch, or another tradition. Sameness was a welcome eighteenth-century quality.

Georgian developed northward as it developed chronologically. Early Georgian reached a zenith in Virginia—at Williamsburg and the great plantation houses of the Tidewater. Throughout the American colonies, however, what is certain is that the goal was less about shelter than what a house looked like, and the more it looked like England the better.

ROBERT CARTER HOUSE, **1750**, Williamsburg, Virginia. Plain yet dignified front; the temple-like porch is a later addition.

PRESIDENT'S HOUSE AT THE COLLEGE OF WILLIAM AND MARY, **1732**, Williamsburg, Virginia.

HOUSE, ca. 1720, Somerset County, New Jersey. / DRAWING: CARTER'S GROVE,
1750–53, James City County, Virginia. Dormer Detail. The house was built by
David Minitree for Carter Burwell. It was probably designed by Richard Taliaferro.

OPPOSITE: **HEYWOOD-WASHINGTON HOUSE**, **ca. 1740**, Charleston, South Carolina. Unadorned five-part facade. /
TOP: **PEYTON RANDOLPH HOUSE**, **1715–18**, Williamsburg, Virginia. Unusual seven-part facade with typical period
monochromatic paint scheme. /**BOTTOM: STEPHEN HOPKINS HOUSE**, **1743**, Providence, Rhode Island.

WENTWORTH-GARDNER HOUSE, **1760**, Portsmouth, New Hampshire. At the end of Early Georgian; has lower roof. Once owned by the Metropolitan Museum, who planned to move the house to Central Park. / **OPPOSITE: HUNTER HOUSE**, **1748**, Newport, Rhode Island.

SAMUEL BARNARD HOUSE, ca. 1758, Deerfield, Massachusetts.

BENJAMIN POWELL HOUSE, ca. 1763, Williamsburg, Virginia.

GENERAL PROPORTIONS

Emphasis on flat symmetrical facade; ideally, the rest of house was rectangular and geometric. Bold in massing and details.

SPATIAL DESIGNATION AND FLOOR PLAN

Primarily two stories, with flat facades and no overhangs. Double-pile plan of central hall with two rooms flanking it on each side.

ROOF TYPES AND FEATURES

Double-pitched gambrel roof remained popular in New England, but gable roof and hipped roofs elsewhere. Dormers. Cornice moldings.

CHIMNEY PLACEMENT

Chimneys move up toward center of the roof.

FENESTRATION

Symmetrical placement of windows, usually in five bays. Overall window proportions still fairly narrow, but double-hung sash with larger panes of glass. No shutters.

ENTRANCEWAY

Centrally placed with raised step. Simple brick or wood lintel; paneled door with simple wood pediment.

STRUCTURAL AND FACEWORK MATERIALS

Mostly frame in New England, brick and some stone elsewhere. House raised on a low base, with water table (Georgian houses do not have gutters). Slightly projecting belt course in wood trim or brick between first and second stories.

COLOR

Wood; colors are generally dark: red, browns, and grays. Masonry houses usually trimmed in reddish brown.

WESTOVER (THE WILLIAM BYRD II MANSION), ca. 1730–34, Charles City County, Virginia. South Door.

MIDDLE GEORGIAN

From the midpoint of the eighteenth century to the American Revolution marks an evolution of the Georgian into far greater sophistication. Style was everything. Proportions became even more classical, and putting stylistic considerations above environmental ones, the pitch of the roofs got lower, while more elaborate plans extended to include flanking wings. The plainer external decoration of Early Georgian was banished in favor of rich external decoration. Doorway treatments, especially, became quite elaborate: segmental, triangular, and swan's neck pediments, as well as fluted pilasters flanking the doorways, were borrowed from English builders' handbooks such as Abraham Swan's *British Architect* (1745, but a Philadelphia edition appeared a few years later).

While there were a few houses built of stone (Cliveden (1763–64) in Philadelphia; Mount Airy (1758–62) in Richmond County, Virginia), many builders carved their wood facades to look like quarried blocks of masonry, while sand was mixed into the paint to create the stonelike texture (George Washington used both techniques when he renovated Mount Vernon (1743–ca. 1780), Virginia). In addition, the corners of houses often received an alternating blocklike treatment in imitation of stone, called quoins. All these details had no other function than decoration.

Monumentality was the aim of the newer style, something achieved by the characteristic Middle Georgian pilasters and columns. Pilasters are applied flat or as half columns that usually adorn the corners and sometimes flank the central bay on either side of the doorway, forming a central pavilion. Governor Horatio Sharpe's Whitehall (ca. 1764–65), near Annapolis, Maryland, was the first house in the colonies to have full-height columns. More common was the columnar double porch, which probably first appeared at Drayton Hall (1738–42), near Charleston, South Carolina, and is exemplified by the Miles Brewton House (1765–69) in the city. The temple form at Whitehall and the double-porch configuration were Palladian in inspiration and were found in books like Gibbs's *A Book of Architecture*.

Palladio and the Neo-Palladians were also the source of the dramatic new five-part plans that were a Middle Georgian hallmark. Whereas Early Georgian houses were pretty much simple rectangular blocks, large Middle Georgian houses sprouted the extended country-house plan of main block with flanking ancillary blocks and connector units. These connectors (sometimes called "hyphens") might be solid (as at Whitehall) or open arcades (as at Mount Vernon); they extended out from the sides of the main block or they curved forward or back. Borrowed almost line for line from the plates in the ubiquitous *A Book of Architecture*, the extended country-house plan was sometimes adapted for an urban setting, such as the Hammond-Harwood (1774), Paca (1763–65), and Bryce (ca. 1770) houses in Annapolis.

The country-house plan was part of the growing wealth of Americans: regardless of size, the plans went hand in hand with the monumental decorative treatments, and the goal was grandeur, or the appearance thereof. And perhaps the most Middle Georgian distinctive decorative device was the Palladian window—the three-part Venetian round-topped window with lower flanking sidelights.

The Middle Georgian house also witnessed increased architectural treatment on the interior. Fireplace surrounds aped the exterior door treatments, while heavy pilasters and entablatures were now painted with bright colors and highlighted. Imported wallpaper and stucco joined the surprisingly bright color schemes. The better Middle Georgian houses were the equals of their London, Bristol, and Dublin equivalents. Just as American furniture, particularly that of Philadelphia and Newport, reached a climax of exceptional artistry and craftsmanship, a house like Mount Pleasant (1761–62), or the Powell House (1764–68), both in Philadelphia, should be recognized as supreme monuments of Anglo-American cultural expression.

OPPOSITE: HOUSE, ca. 1765, Germantown, Pennsylvania. Masonry, splayed lintels, and fancier porch show greater sophistication of Middle Georgian. / TOP: JOSEPH LLOYD MANOR HOUSE, 1767, Lloyd Harbor, New York. / DRAWING (LEFT): MOUNT VERNON, 1757–87, Fairfax County, Virginia. Detail of Palladian window in the great banquet room, a remodeling ca. 1776–77. / DRAWING (RIGHT): WENTWORTH-GARDNER HOUSE, 1760, Portsmouth, New Hampshire. Detail of quoins.

TOP: **HAMILTON HOUSE**, **ca. 1785**, South Berwick, Maine. Col. Jonathan Hamilton, Architect. Restored ca. 1900 by Herbert Brown, this shipbuilder's home is a classic Middle Georgian house of the Piscataqua region. / BOTTOM: **VASSALL-LONGFELLOW HOUSE**, **ca. 1759**, Cambridge, Massachusetts. / OPPOSITE: **MILES BREWTON HOUSE**, **1765–9**, Charleston, South Carolina. Double-height Palladian portico.

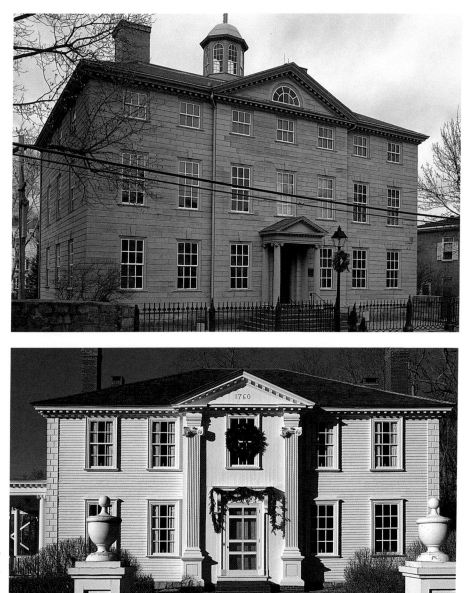

JOSEPH JENCKES HOUSE, 1773, Providence, Rhode Island. / **DRAWING: HAMMOND-HARWOOD HOUSE**, 1773–74, Annapolis, Maryland. William Buckland, Architect.

GENERAL PROPORTIONS

Symmetrical front facades with boxlike, cubic configuration behind.

SPATIAL DESIGNATION AND FLOOR PLAN

Main block usually rectangular. Country house versions feature five-part Palladian plan of main block, flanking wings, and connectors.

ROOF TYPE AND FEATURES

Pitch lower than Early Georgian. Dormers. Balustrades at top of roof (some balustrades have Chinese detailing).

CHIMNEY PLACEMENT

Chimneys move closer to center of house (up the roof to break in pitch), particularly on hipped roofs (symmetry supplanting practicality in the grander examples).

FENESTRATION

Symmetrical bays, usually five, sometimes seven. Window panes are larger and overall shape of window is rectangular to square. Palladian windows.

ENTRANCEWAY

Central pavilions. Pediments. Double porches (one above the other). Full-height columns and pilasters.

STRUCTURAL AND FACEWORK MATERIALS

Masonry, timber, and occasionally stone. Wood carved to look like stone. Shutters. Quoins on corners.

COLOR

Wood houses were usually painted white with a linseed oil-based yellow cast; sometimes light gray or pale blue, and often with strongly contrasting trim. Some brightly colored high-style houses. Shutters dark green.

GOVERNOR LANGDON HOUSE, **1784**, Portsmouth, New Hampshire. Dormer detail.

LATE GEORGIAN

Independence from the mother country did not mean an end to the Georgian style. Far from cutting ties to Britain, American architectural tastes were, if anything, just as English as before. Americans (some of whose new states retained the shilling as their unit of currency) did not substitute another style for the Georgian. Rather, there was a flowering of the Late Georgian. It has long been fashionable to refer to the era following the American Revolution as the Federal Period, but it is more helpful to label its design as Late Georgian.

Styles historically evolve from experimental early development to a classic moment and on to a time of decline (Greek art with its Archaic, Classical, and Hellenistic phases, for example). So, the Federal style was the Georgian's last, richest, and even decadent chapter. As with the Hellenistic, the blockier forms of Early Georgian and the balanced ones of the Middle Georgian were replaced by more graceful, more attenuated, less bold, and less vigorous forms. All the decorative elements became thinner: pilasters, columns, mullions; delicacy was the watchword: wall surfaces, whether wood or brick, became flatter, with fewer shadows.

In England, the archaeological discoveries of Late Roman styles at Herculaneum and Pompeii (both cities had been buried by the 79 A.D. eruption of Mount Vesuvius) introduced a delicate antidote to the heavy English Baroque and ascetic Neo-Palladianism. The English gentleman's educational walkabout on the continent called the grand tour was still very much in vogue. The publications of Palladio and Inigo Jones were pushed aside by those of the Scottish architect Robert Adam (1728–1792) with his studies of Late Roman domestic design. Thus, Late Georgian deservedly carries the sobriquet of Adamesque.

One of America's first professional architects, Charles Bulfinch (1763–1844), returned from England with the goal of transforming his native Boston from a provincial capital into a reflection of Adamesque London. The President's House (1795–1797) in Philadelphia was a brick cube that would not have looked out of place in Mayfair, while its successor, the White House (designed 1792), in Washington, D.C., was based on a public building in Dublin, although its details were Adamesque. Even Thomas Jefferson's house (begun 1768) at Monticello, Virginia, owes much to Anglo-Roman models.

As happened with the transition from Early to Middle Georgian, roof pitches got even lower (so much for snowfall in New England—style comes first), sometimes disappearing behind balustrades. Basic geometric forms became attenuated, even mannered, with square rooms often replaced by lozenge-shaped or oval rooms (hence the White House's Oval Office); segmental and elliptical fanlights, with lace-thin lead tracery, made pre-Revolutionary door treatments seem stockier, more masculine by comparison. The bright colors of the Middle Georgian were replaced with pastels; urns seen in the mosaics of Pompeii appeared on both balustrades and furniture. Grace aptly describes the best Late Georgian design.

The five-part English country-house plans of the Middle Georgian persisted, (compare Whitehall with Baltimore's Homewood (1801), and they seem identical except for delicacy of details and the flatness of the masonry). The Late Georgian flourished in Charleston and especially along the New England coast in those Federalist strongholds that opposed Mr. Jefferson's War of 1812. For a few glorious years, China trade ports such as Salem and Newburyport in Massachusetts, and Wiscasset in Maine, were among the wealthiest towns in the nation. Along London-like squares and elm-lined streets, cubic houses with nearly flat roofs, thin columns, and achingly beautiful fanlights created the swansong of the Georgian style.

Builders' handbooks like Connecticut-born architect Asher Benjamin's *The Country Builder's Assistant* of 1797 spread the Late Georgian into the interior of New England, across New York State, and on to Ohio and Kentucky. But subsequent popular books, such as Benjamin's *American Builder's Companion*, whose 1806 edition carried Greek details, would spell doom for the Georgian.

GARDNER-PINGREE HOUSE, 1804–06, Salem, Massachusetts. Front elevation. By Samuel McIntire for John Gardner. The Fence, modeled after Pl. 54 in Asher Benjamin's *Complete Builder's Guide,* was added in 1840. / **OPPOSITE: FRENCH'S TAVERN, CA. 1812**, Dublin, New Hampshire. Rural carpenter's sophistication, naive yet elegant.

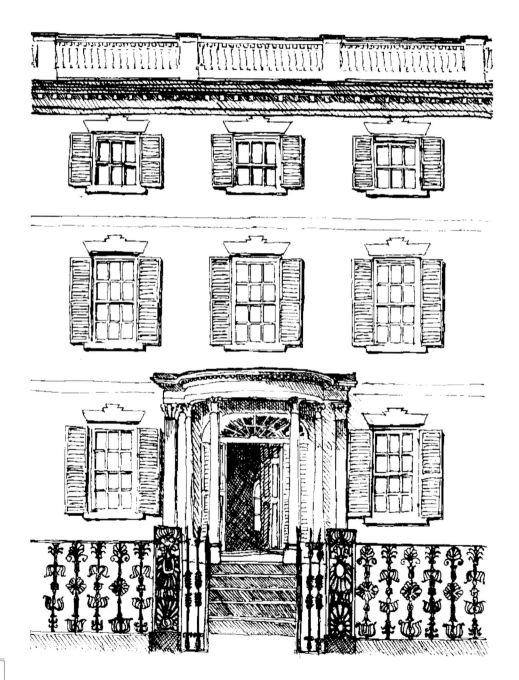

TOP: FORREST HALL, ca. 1800, New Ipswich, New Hampshire. Built as a wedding gift for Charles Barrett; movie based on Henry James's *The Europeans* was filmed here. / **BOTTOM: THOMAS LLOYD HALSEY HOUSE, ca. 1800**, Providence, Rhode Island. Fancy double-bow house built by a successful China trader.

GARDNER-PINGREE HOUSE, **1804–06**, Salem, Massachusetts. Columns detail.

OPPOSITE: **NATHANIEL RUSSELL HOUSE**, **ca. 1803**, Charleston, South Carolina. Russell Warren, Architect. Shallow arches, roof hidden behind balustrade, and semi-octagonal room to side. / **ELI SMALLWOOD HOUSE**, **ca. 1810**, New Bern, North Carolina. Delicate front door columns in colonial capital of North Carolina.

FARMINGTON, **ca. 1815**, Louisville, Kentucky. Attributed to Thomas Jefferson and certainly a relative of Virginia homes by the architect-president. / **DRAWING: FORMAN HOUSE, 1812**, Syracuse, New York. Doorway detail.

TOP: **OWEN-THOMAS HOUSE**, **ca. 1817**, Savannah, Georgia. William Jay, Architect.
American version of English Regency. / BOTTOM: **HOUSE**, **ca. 1830**, Savannah, Georgia.

GENERAL PROPORTIONS

Symmetry. Details more delicate; proportions more refined and elegant.

SPATIAL DESIGNATION AND FLOOR PLAN

Two and three stories, with second story not as tall as the first, and the third not as tall as the second. Double-pile plan with addition of oval and elliptical walls of rooms. Bow fronts. In the South, prominent projecting pavilions, double porches, or full-height porticos.

ROOF TYPES AND FEATURES

Hipped roofs, considerably lower than in Middle Georgian. Balustrade, often with Roman urns, either at ridge or on the edge of the roof (which makes roof virtually invisible).

CHIMNEY PLACEMENT

Slenderer chimneys.

FENESTRATION

Large panes in six-over-six configuration. Windows set in shallow recessed arches. Palladian windows. Elliptical windows; round-headed windows with curved tracery.

ENTRANCEWAY

Porticos (South) and small, sometimes elliptical, porches. Central doorway topped by semicircular or semi-elliptical fanlight; doors flanked by narrow vertical sidelights. Slender columns and/or pilasters.

STRUCTURAL AND FACEWORK MATERIALS

Brick and frame, with wood porches, balustrades, columns, and pilasters. Bowed facades (brick). Delicate, low relief (or nearly flat) decorative ornament (swags, flowers, urns, bouquets).

COLOR

Lighter, more pastel colors; brick could be painted. Lots of white or off-white houses; some dark green ones. Shutters dark green.

TRUMAN BECKWITH HOUSE, **1826**, Providence, Rhode Island. John Holden Greene, Architect.

03

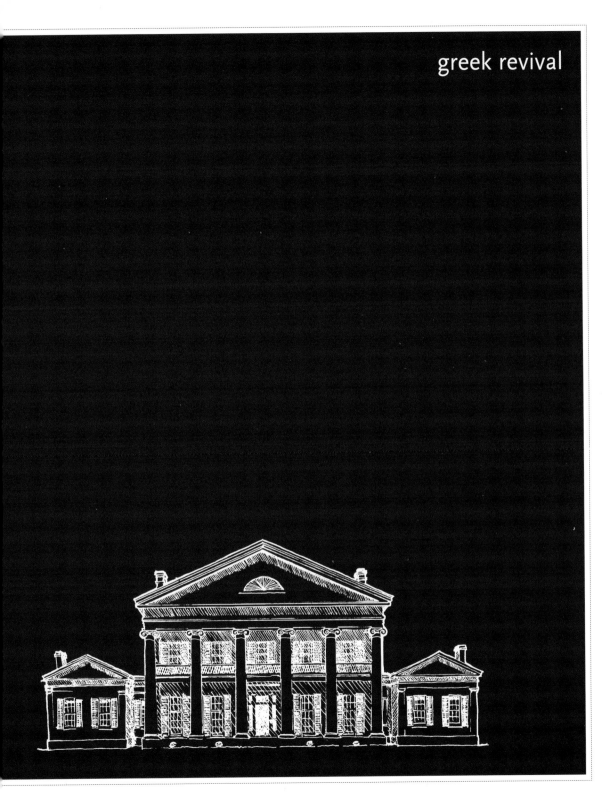

GREEK REVIVAL IMPLIES A STYLE BOTH PUBLIC AND MONUMENTAL. Although handsome, Georgian was a domestic style—even large civic buildings like Independence Hall were basically overscaled houses. Greek Revival houses, while often no larger than their English-inspired predecessors, bore the mantle of classicism: columns, temple forms, porticoes, and a definite historical presence.

It is tempting to attribute the success of the Greek Revival in the United States to national identification with Greece as the birthplace of democracy. The Greek war of independence from the Turks during the 1820s may have mirrored our own earlier struggles and offered a Romantic model. The proliferation of classical place names throughout the country, but especially in New York—Athens, Troy, Sparta, Syracuse— may be further proof of our interest in the world of the ancients. The Greek mode was equally popular throughout Europe, so we were hardly unique. Is a school in Edinburgh, a church in Copenhagen, or an art museum in Berlin, as much a temple of democracy as a state capitol in the American Midwest?

Delightful though it may be to think of settlers carving out a town from the Kentucky forest or the Indiana prairie and declaring their home as the new Corinth or Utica, the success of the Greek as a domestic style was more a product of fashion than politics, history, or Romantic musings. As we have already seen with Georgian, fashion is almost everything, and Greek was the new rage. While it may have suitably expressed Jacksonian democracy, Americans embraced the Greek because it looked good: a temple-form house with columns made the right statement.

There were books that carried correct Greek orders, but the simplest way to create an example of the new classicism was to turn the gable end of a house to the front. Suitably pitched, the gable end became a pediment. Add corner pilasters, heavier door and window surrounds (all created darker shadow lines and made the home seem more substantial, more serious), and a simple farmhouse became stylish. If there was enough money, a portico or maybe just a porch supported by a couple of columns was attached.

Of the three Greek orders—Doric, Ionic, and Corinthian—the Doric was the simplest to make and it had the virtue of looking more masculine and less delicate (in contrast to the slender columns of the Late Georgian); even square columns could transform a home into a temple. American housebuilders may have admired Greek architecture, but they were happy to borrow the styles or forms that they liked and that were easily fashioned. As a three-columned portico on a Connecticut Valley farmhouse demonstrates, the canons of classical design were not taken too seriously.

Whether elaborate temples, complete with columns and archaeologically correct entablatures, or just simple rectangular houses with a few details recalling an Aegean temple, the Greek Revival house represented a period of unprecedented prosperity. A temple in Vermont marked the success of a sheep farmer, while Greek Revival houses in Ohio's Western Reserve showed that the new settlers were planning to set down roots for the ages. But it was in the Deep South, especially in the plantation country of Georgia, Alabama, Mississippi, and Louisiana, where the Greek Revival achieved its finest expression. For many, the Greek Revival house with a giant portico, often stretching completely around the house, *is* the antebellum South.

OPPOSITE: **HOUSE**, **1833**, Newport, Rhode Island. / **BELOW TOP: CAPTAIN FRANCIS WEST HOUSE**, **1834**, Essex, Connecticut. / **BELOW BOTTOM: HOUSE**, **ca. 1836**, Chicago, Illinois. Farmhouse as temple: classical pilasters, porch, doorway, and tower.

HOUSE, ca. 1830, Princeton, New Jersey. Charles Steadman, Architect. Elaborate doorway treatment on a simple frame house. Greek palmettes on iron fence. / **OPPOSITE, TOP: CHARLES Q. CLAPP HOUSE, 1832**, Portland, Maine. Inventive temple treatment with corner columns. / **BOTTOM: WILLIAM ROTCH RODMAN HOUSE, 1833**, New Bedford, Massachusetts. Massive Corinthian columns and stone masonry are a tribute to the great wealth of this whaling port.

TOP: **STEPHENS-BLACK HOUSE**, **ca. 1837**, Staten Island, New York. Farmhouse Greek. / BOTTOM: **SMITH-ROURKE HOUSE**, **ca. 1837**, East Patchogue, New York. Captain William Smith, Jr., Builder. Pediment on tower matches that on main block of the house. / OPPOSITE: **ELIZA ANN JEWETT HOUSE**, **1842**, Savannah, Georgia. Greek applied to an in-town house.

KERRISON HOUSE, **ca. 1838**, Charleston, South Carolina. Elegance and dignity of a full-height portico.

GAINESWOOD, ca. 1842, Demopolis, Alabama. Nathan Bryan Whitfield, Architect.
Handsome, austere, proportionally beautiful. Plantation Greek at its best. /
DRAWING: ANDALUSIA, 1798, Philadelphia, Pennsylvania. Column detail.

OPPOSITE: **MILO MASON HOUSE**, **1843**, Providence, Rhode Island. / **AVERY-DOWNER HOUSE**, **1842**, Granville, Ohio. Benjamin Morgan, Architect. Ambitious Greek exercise with Ionic temple front, Doric side temples, and a giant acroterion at the peak of the main gable.

WESSELL-HARPER HOUSE, ca. 1846, Wilmington, North Carolina.

TOP: **HOUSE, ca. 1850**, Marlborough, New Hampshire. / **BOTTOM:**
RICHARD HEYWOOD HOUSE, ca. 1854, Raleigh, North Carolina.
Richard Heywood, Architect.

LEWIS-SMITH HOUSE, ca. 1855, Raleigh, North Carolina.

MOSER HOUSE, **1875**, Galveston, Texas. John Hourigan, Architect. Greek temple forms hang on long after the style itself has gone out of fashion.

TOP: **HOUSE**, **ca. 1845**, Northfield, Massachusetts. That virtually no Greek temple sources had three columns did not appear to bother the builder of this Connecticut Valley house. / BOTTOM: **SHELDON HOUSE**, **ca. 1835–50**, Princeton, New Jersey. Moved from Northampton, Massachusetts, by barge in 1868. / OPPOSITE: **RUSSELL HOUSE**, **ca. 1828–30**, Middletown, Connecticut. Alexander Jackson Davis, Architect. A temple by one of the style's great temple builders.

greek revival notes on the defining characteristics

GENERAL PROPORTIONS

Rectangular blocks; temple-form massing.

ROOF TYPES AND FEATURES

A simple gable, with low pitch, reflecting rake of the pedimented end. Roof may not be visible in larger example or behind cornice and parapet. In peripteral examples (columns extending along three sides or around the house), the roof is hipped. No dormers.

FENESTRATION

Windows are universally trabeated, that is, with flat lintels. Six-over-six windows, with ground-floor windows often taller than second-story windows. Three-story examples often have half or considerably smaller attic windows. Window surrounds can be quite heavy, with entablatures and details that imitate the main entablature of the house.

STRUCTURAL AND FACEWORK MATERIALS

Brick, wood, and masonry walls, with wood being the most common. Details, such as columns, entablatures, and window frames almost always wood.

SPATIAL DESIGNATION AND FLOOR PLAN

Usually one and a half to two main stories (attic story in urban versions). Rectangular temple form plans, often with ell-shaped wings to one side or both sides of main block. Gable end faces the street. Larger examples have entrance in center, while the entrance is often to the side in smaller, three-bay versions. Temple form may be a simple pediment or pediment with a complete classical entablature above a columned portico. A fan in the gable end is often found in vernacular examples. Corner pilasters.

CHIMNEY PLACEMENT

Slender chimneys at the eaves; chimneys often not visible from the front.

ENTRANCEWAY ATTRIBUTES

Even the plainest of examples will have flanking pilasters, but doorways can be quite elaborate, with engaged columns, sidelights, transoms, and entablatures composed of Greek frets, palmettes, and acroteria at the corners. A recessed doorway, with columns, especially Doric and set in antis, was also popular.

COLOR

Historically, most were white when built, with dark green shutters.

MADEWOOD, 1846–48, near Napoleonville, Louisiana. Front elevation. The house was designed by Henry Howard for Thomas Pugh.

04

gothic revival

THE SAME ROMANTIC IMPULSE THAT FAVORED the Greek temple as a house type also advanced the Gothic Revival. The idea of a Gothic house seems like an anomaly, as one usually thinks of Gothic as the style of the great cathedrals of the Middle Ages, best known as a style for churches and colleges in this country. While Medieval might naturally seem to be the exact opposite of classical—darkness versus light, religious mysticism rather than humanistic clarity—the choice to clothe one's dwelling in a particular style was more a function of fashion than of philosophical or religious belief. The Gothic exerted a strong fascination for homebuilders and the result was some of our most delightful houses.

Gothic forms—pointed arches, castellated battlements, and picturesque rooflines—were revived more slowly than Roman and Greek Revival ones. Gothic was not as exotic as the bygone Age of Pericles; besides, northern Europeans had grown up with medieval buildings all around them. While other English noblemen were wandering in Italy, Sir Horace Walpole wrote the first Gothic novel, at the same time transforming his country estate with parapets, towers, and drip moldings. Subsequently, the novels of Scottish writer Sir Walter Scott fueled the passion for the Romantic past of ruined monasteries, knights in armor, and moonlit graveyards. Builders' guides began to include Gothic details, and as early as 1799, architect Benjamin Henry Latrobe (1764–1820) (the architect of the U.S. Capitol and creator of the first American building with a correct Greek order) built a house outside of Philadelphia that had pointed arches and window moldings in the Gothic style.

The Gothic Revival's champion on the domestic front was the immensely popular tastemaker-architect Andrew Jackson Downing (1815–1852). This Hudson River valley nurseryman, horticulturist, and landscape architect wrote some of the most successful instructional guidebooks ever. Titles such as *Cottage Residences* of 1842 and *The Architecture of Country Houses*, published in 1850, made English theoretical writings on the picturesque understandable to the average reader and interested Americans in their houses as never before. The books were inexpensive, persuasively written, and offered advice and house plans so that middle-class Americans could build evocative and Picturesque *cottages*. Downing detested Greek and argued that temples were not suited to contemporary American homes; Downing even showed how one might update a Greek or Georgian house and make it fashionably Gothic.

It is difficult to overestimate the influence of the handsome and dashing Downing. And while Americans have always shown a reluctance to follow rules, they took his stylistic teachings to heart. Coupled with the development of scroll saws, ornate decoration could now be produced economically, so houses across the country began to sport "gingerbread" on bargeboards, porch columns, and peaked gables. The Gothic cottage did not need to be symmetrical (as a Greek temple did), and it could be enlarged or expanded without fear of losing its picturesque qualities. Some architects created notable stone castles and cottages that accurately duplicated the plates in Downing's books. But countless Americans simply made Gothic houses by building taller, narrow houses, sometimes with a peaked gable above the front porch. It was this vernacular version that carried the style south and westward (the house in the background of American Regionalist painter Grant Wood's iconic work *American Gothic* (1930) is one of those cottages, featuring vertical board-and-batten siding and a pointed-arch window) until it became ubiquitous.

After the Civil War, equally romantic but even more picturesque house styles would replace the simple Gothic cottage. Gothic would return later in the castles of the robber barons, but the cottages of the 1840s and 1850s constitute a particularly democratic chapter in American house building.

OPPOSITE: **ROTCH HOUSE**, **1845**, New Bedford, Massachusetts. Alexander Jackson Davis, Architect. The iconic Gothic Revival Cottage, built at the height of whaling industry. / **ASHE COTTAGE**, **ca. 1850**, Demopolis, Alabama. Dr. William Cincinnatus Ashe, Architect. Downing cottage with twin gables; note unusual "running" bargeboard.

WALLACE CARPENTER HOUSE, **1855**, Granville, Ohio. Wallace Carpenter, Architect.

Small house Gothicized with crenellated battlements and flat Tudor arches.

OAKWOOD, **1851**, Newark, Ohio. Alexander Jackson Davis, Architect.
America's premier Gothic cottage designer's work reached the Midwest.

EVANS-HOLTON-OWENS HOUSE, ca. 1850, Newark, Ohio. / DRAWING:
LUCIAN K. SMITH HOUSE, 1863, Black Hawk, Colorado. Gable detail. /
OPPOSITE: ROGERS HOUSE, ca. 1850, Granville, Ohio.

DAVID W. HOYT HOUSE, **1877**, Providence, Rhode Island.

HOUSE, **1845**, Peterborough, New Hampshire. Taken right from a plate in one of Downing's books.

BOWEN HOUSE/ROSELAND COTTAGE, **1846**, Woodstock, Connecticut. "Roseland" was built as a summer house by Hendry Chandler Bowen, a Woodstock native who made it big in New York City. / **OPPOSITE: CUTTER HOUSE**, **1856**, Minneapolis, Minnesota.

gothic revival notes on the defining characteristics

GENERAL PROPORTIONS

Verticality emphasized, with picturesque outlines.

ROOF TYPES AND FEATURES

Rooflines are complicated and picturesque. Steeply pitched gable roofs are the norm, with one or several intersecting gables. Ridges may have cast iron cresting and finials. Wood shingles predominate, but many examples have patterned roofs of slate.

FENESTRATION

Tall, narrow, and glazed with diamond-shaped panes, often polygonal and placed in projecting bays (upper-story windows are often set in self-contained projecting oriels). Window openings are outlined by a variety of moldings in the shape of Gothic arches or nearly flat Tudor, the more pointed ogee, and triangular arches.

STRUCTURAL AND FACEWORK MATERIALS

May be brick or stone, but the majority are wood (some wood houses are designed to look like masonry). Siding often is vertical board and batten. Bargeboards decorate the insides of the steeply pitched eaves of both roofs and dormers. Similar elaborate carvings may be added to porch railings and cornices. Gables are tall and steeply pitched.

SPATIAL DESIGNATION AND FLOOR PLAN

Usually a story and a half or two stories tall, with exceptions in urban examples or in castle-sized estates. Plans are usually asymmetrical, although some houses have central hallways with flanking rooms, and almost none are simple rectangular shapes. Porches can run along an entire facade, but several smaller porches are more typical.

CHIMNEY PLACEMENT

Chimneys are often made of patterned terra-cotta pipes ganged together in pairs and placed off center. Chimneys were seen as important decorative accents.

ENTRANCEWAY ATTRIBUTES

Gothic doorways are invariably set beneath one-story porches, whether simple or elaborate. The doors themselves may be arched (or have arched transoms) and paneled with recessed arch patterns.

COLOR

There is a tendency toward earth tones: tan (Downing's "quiet fawn colour"), brown, gray, and sometimes red or dark brown. Details are best, in Downing's words, "painted in several shades darker. . . of the main colour."

HENRY DELAMATER HOUSE, 1844, Rhinebeck, New York. Front elevation. Alexander Jackson Davis, Architect.

05

THE ITALIANATE IS ANOTHER OF THE ROMANTIC FASHIONS that swept American house design in the decades before the Civil War. But unlike the classical temples and Gothic castles, the primary source for the Italian villa was domestic.

Italy exerted a profound draw for American literati in the nineteenth century (just as it had for the English the century before). Nathaniel Hawthorne, Henry Wadsworth Longfellow, and James Fenimore Cooper all were enchanted by Roman ruins and wandered the countryside. American painters and sculptors, too—Samuel Morse, Frederick Church, and John Vanderlyn, Horatio Greenough, and Harriet Hosmer—were so inspired by Italy that they moved there to work.

The house that symbolized this love of all things Italian was not a Renaissance city palace or a great villa of the time of Hadrian: it was the late-medieval fortified farmhouses from the hilly Tuscan countryside around Florence that inspired the new fashion. Much less pretentious than the in-town palazzi with their proportional and cultured facades, the country houses were more practical. Best of all, many of these comfortable farmhouses retained their vestigial fortified towers, which became places from which to take in views of the landscape.

When the Italian country-house style appeared in England in 1802, the tower remained a prominent feature, along with smooth stucco walls, nearly flat roofs, asymmetrical plans, and piazzas. The open piazza or loggia (often with an arcade of rounded columns familiar to lovers of Early Renaissance Annunciation paintings) was both the fashion's hallmark and its great advantage: it encouraged a relatively casual style of living, uniting indoors and out. And, as so often happens, royal patronage boosted the style's popularity. The Prince Regent (later George IV), and his primary architect, John Nash (1752–1835), injected an Italian flavor into their Regency-style seaside villas. George's niece, Victoria, and her husband, Albert, embraced the full-blown Tuscan-villa aesthetic in building their favorite home, Osborne House on the Isle of Wight.

Of greater significance to Americans was the fact that Andrew Jackson Downing included Italianate models in his influential house books. Architects such as A. J. Davis (1803–1892), John Notman (1810–1865), and Richard Upjohn (1803–1878) contributed designs to Downing; one Upjohn plate in *Country Residences* is similar to Italianate houses he built in Newport, Rhode Island, and Baltimore, Maryland.

Towers often appeared on the North American version of the Tuscan villa, usually with a pair or trio of round-arched windows (the medieval fortified house was Romanesque not Gothic), and invariably featured a piazza—what we simply call a porch. Ideally, the porch wrapped around two or more sides of a house and extended the living space outside, particularly in warm weather. Extra-tall windows increased this interior-exterior circulation, while both porch and fenestration reflected the openness of the plan within. Instead of the usual four-room block of the Georgian or the hall and side-room plan of the Greek, the Tuscan house was more fluid, with spaces flowing easily between rooms. This casual arrangement would have important ramifications in the development of the Queen Anne and Shingle styles.

The towered houses usually have L-shaped plans, but smaller towers are placed in the center of squarer versions of the style. Italianate was especially popular in urban townhouse form, where its elaborate cornices graced brownstones' facades.

Italianate bespoke elegance. Its round windows seemingly smiled, while the door-like windows opening on to the porch suggested social intercourse—a place from which to view a meadow or the ocean.

OPPOSITE: **HANCHETT-BARTLETT HOMESTEAD**, **1857**, Beloit, Wisconsin. James Hanchett, Architect. Long ground-floor windows and prominent roof with belvedere bring Italy to southern Wisconsin. / TOP: **CENTRAL GEORGIA RAILROAD HOUSE**, **1875**, Savannah, Georgia. Augustus Schwab, Architect. / BOTTOM: **HUGH MERCER HOUSE**, **1871**, Savannah, Georgia. Muller and Bruyn, Architects.

W. B. BLADES HOUSE, ca. 1903, New Bern, North Carolina. Herbert W. Simpson, Architect.

J. S. A. ASHE HOUSE, **ca. 1853**, Charleston, South Carolina. A Florentine arcade, or piazza, lends itself to capturing sea breezes.

OPPOSITE: ROBERT LIPPITT HOUSE, 1854, Providence, Rhode Island. Thomas Tefft, Architect. Italian Renaissance palazzo: stern, dignified, relying upon massing more than ornament. / **ANDREWS-DUNCAN HOUSE, 1874**, Raleigh, North Carolina. G. S. H. Appleget, Architect.

OPPOSITE: **ORTMAN-SCHUMATE HOUSE**, **1870**, San Francisco, California. San Francisco developed an appropriately urban row house version of the Italianate. / **FISK HOUSE**, **ca. 1870**, Minneapolis, Minnesota.

CLARENCE H. CARPENTER HOUSE, **1872**, Providence, Rhode Island. Even without the classic Tuscan tower, Italianate houses exhibit an urbane presence.

PIPER PRICE HOUSE, **1854**, Philadelphia, Pennsylvania. Samuel Sloan, Architect.

Sloan published popular pattern books on the Italianate.

OPPOSITE: **MITCHELL HOUSE**, **1856**, Philadelphia, Pennsylvania. / **HOUSE**, **ca. 1855**, Bennington, Vermont. Bracket detail.

ELMINGTON, **1865**, Newport, Rhode Island. Verandas for catching sea breezes.

JAMES TAYLOR HOUSE, **1859**, New Bedford, Massachusetts. Renaissance palace in wood; framed with giant pilasters.

italianate notes on the defining characteristics

GENERAL PROPORTIONS

Cubic masses, often asymmetrical. Square towers.

ROOF TYPES AND FEATURES

Very low-pitched roof supported by bracketed, prominently projecting eaves; brackets usually in pairs.

FENESTRATION

Round-arched windows in pairs. Ground-floor windows often reach to floor level, while windows in the tower are characteristically grouped in threes.

STRUCTURAL AND FACEWORK MATERIALS

Examples in wood, brick, or stone exist, but the ideal material is heavily-scored masonry or brick covered with a stucco finish.

SPATIAL DESIGNATION AND FLOOR PLAN

Blocky, rectangular units with wings creating L-shaped plans. Urban houses are taller and with less variations, but the freestanding Italianate villa offers both a sense of verticality with its centrally placed or offset tower, and that of horizontality with its two-story blocks wrapped by verandas.

CHIMNEY PLACEMENT

Tall, smooth, massive chimneys, asymmetrically placed.

ENTRANCEWAY ATTRIBUTES

The main entrance door is paneled and double type, and can have either a flat, if decorated, lintel above or a rounded transom. Doorway is in the tower block, especially if the tower is in the center of the composition.

COLOR

Masonry left in natural state, or wood and brick painted to approximate colors of stone: tans, browns, grays, with contrasting trim color that pretty much follows Downing's color recommendations.

LINCOLN-TALLMAN HOUSE, 1857, Janesville, Wisconsin. Heavy moldings, quoins, bracketed
cornice, and belvedere on the roof create sophisticated Tuscan air.

THE SECOND EMPIRE REVIVAL WAS ANOTHER OF THOSE hugely popular house styles with thoroughly European roots. The mansard roofs, tall floors, and heavy moldings of the Second Empire house became so ubiquitous that no one would question the subject of Edward Hopper's painting *House by the Railroad* (1925) or the mansion-homestead of the vast Riata ranching empire in the film *Giant* (1956) as anything else than quintessentially nineteenth-century Americana. As with other styles we borrowed, we transformed them into something quite our own.

Almost as confusing as the fact that an urbane and urban style would be so wholeheartedly embraced by everyday American homebuilders, is the name itself. The empire referred to was that of Napoléon III (ruled as emperor of the French, 1852–71), nephew of Napoléon I. Louis-Napoléon (as the second emperor was called) who was not remembered for his military prowess but for the rebuilding of Paris into the City of Light—an impressive modern capital with grand boulevards lined by public monuments and townhouses, all wearing mansard roofs. Never mind that the nearly vertical roof form had been advanced in the seventeenth century by architect François Mansart, who popularized the style (his grandnephew Jules Hardouin-Mansart later worked for Louis XIV); the mansard was almost as stylish as Emperor Napoléon III's consort, Eugénie. The empress did not control a generation's aesthetic destiny, but her celebrity helped the fashion's acceptance here.

Parisian or not, the Second Empire style became virtually an American national style, especially for civic buildings. During its height, almost every courthouse and post office and many a city hall carried the style's characteristic Classicistic-Baroque decorative devices of paired columns, *œuil de boeuf* (bull's-eye) windows, and mansard roofs squared into domes. It was the mansard that transferred so easily to the American house and that gave the Second Empire its most recognizable hallmark.

Except for the roof forms, the Second Empire house was not all that different from the Italianate villas that preceded it. Given the more formal classical sources, however, the facades were more likely to be symmetrical, while the tower was often moved to the center of the composition. The porch is still very much a key feature, while the round-arched windows have heavier moldings, and more elaborate brackets replaced the simpler paired ones of the Italianate villa. In the 1870s, the mansards were often shingled in contrasting patterns, and the rooflines and towers were topped with spiky iron crestings, giving the whole a more Victorian quality—the haunted house made famous by the *New Yorker* cartoonist Charles Addams.

By the end of its hugely successful run, Second Empire houses added more and more colors—where did Parisian taste end and Victorian Gothic begin? Inside, one thinks of a house like this as dark and lugubrious, with heavy curtains, mahogany furniture, and a suitably Victorian family gathered around a heavy marble fireplace. Nevertheless, the style was found from Maine to California, for Second Empire was comfortable, practical (roofs are usually cheaper to build than walls), and offered a dash of elegance.

OPPOSITE: HULL PLACE, **1875**, Newark, Ohio. Quoins, mansard, and heavy yet fanciful window moldings. /
EDWARD H. SWAN HOUSE, **1872**, Oyster Bay, New York. John W. Ritch, Architect. Paris on Long Island.

DRAWING: **HOUSE**, **ca. 1860**, Troy, New York. Quoins detail. / **BOTTOM: GILBERT RUSSELL HOUSE**, **ca. 1880**, New Bedford, Massachusetts. When decoration becomes overly whimsical and over-the-top. / **OPPOSITE: PETER RHOADES HOUSE**, **ca. 1850**, Newark, Ohio. Second Empire was popular everywhere in the United States.

HOUSE, Wilmington, North Carolina. / **OPPOSITE: WHEELER-KOHN HOUSE**, 1870, Chicago, Illinois. Otis Wheelock, Architect. / **DRAWING: HOUSE**, ca. 1865, Waterford, New York. Tower detail.

HOUSE, ca. 1870, Princeton, New Jersey. / **OPPOSITE, TOP: JOHN O. SMITH HOUSE**, 1881, Savannah, Georgia. / **BOTTOM: BURDICK HOUSE**, 1876, Providence, Rhode Island. Even a cottage-sized Second Empire provides dignity and presence.

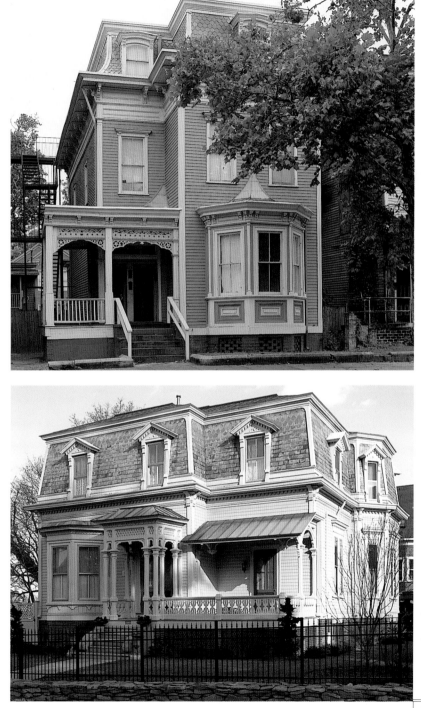

OPPOSITE: SPRAGUE HOUSE, **1867**, Red Wing, Minnesota. Although details are classic Second Empire, tower, porch, and plan show the style's debt to Italianate. / **MARTIN-HUGGINS HOUSE**, **1870**, Wilmington, North Carolina. James F. Post, Architect.

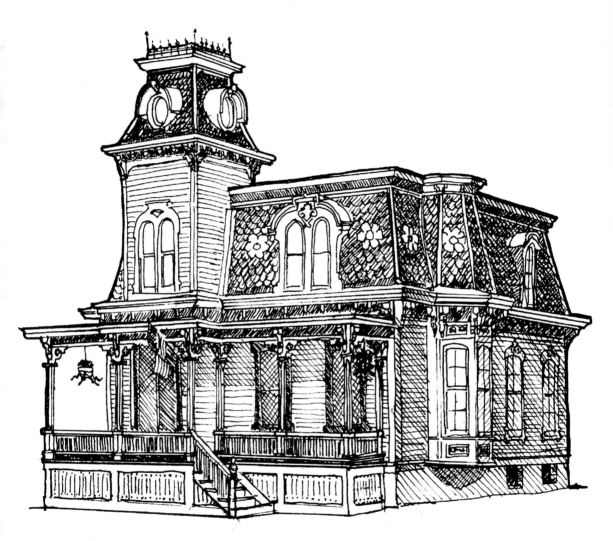

GENERAL PROPORTIONS

Classical rectangular blocks with second or third story comprised of almost vertical roof. Examples with towers read as especially vertical.

ROOF TYPES AND FEATURES

The most characteristic feature is the mansard roof. The mansard is nearly vertical (can be concave, convex, or straight) and forms the second or third story of the typical example. A mansard covers the centrally placed tower. Roofs are covered with slates in decorative fish-scale patterns, sometimes in contrasting colors. Cast-iron crestings line the top of the mansards. Dormers are ubiquitous and often heavily decorated.

FENESTRATION

Windows are usually two-over-two double-hung sash with rounded or segmental arched tops. Window surrounds can range from classical to heavy drip moldings. First-floor windows often reach floor level. Semi-octagonal bays are common, as are heavy framed dormers.

STRUCTURAL AND FACEWORK MATERIALS

The majority are of wood, though there are major examples in stone, and many in brick. Walls are clapboard and substantial quoins are common.

SPATIAL DESIGNATION AND FLOOR PLAN

Formal, rectangular, and, for the most part, symmetrical blocks with central, on-axis doorways, towers, and hallways. Porches across front facade of house, often with smaller porches on sides and backs.

CHIMNEY PLACEMENT

Much more prominent and substantial than, for instance, the clay flues of the Gothic; the stacks have enlarged caps and can be placed at roof edges or toward the center (often in pairs, flanking the central tower).

ENTRANCEWAY ATTRIBUTES

Heavy double doors with segmental or round-arch transoms. Main doorway treatments can be quite heavy, oftentimes with stone *voussoirs*, but more typically porches supported by paired or ganged columns, as well as elaborate brackets.

COLOR

Colors range from the natural tones of stone and masonry to bright color combinations (made of tertiary colors, such as olive and russet), often with contrasting highlights. Sample palettes could include medium olive or straw with dark olive trim; dark blue body colors with brownstone and fawn.

P.Q. WATSON HOUSE, **ca. 1865**, Lloyd Harbor, New York. The house's glory is its iron-crested railing.

victorian

stick style

queen anne

richardsonian

shingle style

VICTORIAN: AN OVERVIEW

Victorian is as broad a term as *Colonial*. It is also so ingrained in our cultural vocabulary that it would be equally hard to exorcise. For many Americans, Victorian is synonymous with bad taste (architecture critic Lewis Mumford (1895–1990) referred to the age as the "Brown Decades"), and for far too long merely attaching the label to an older house was enough to spell its doom. Tastes fortunately do change, and what was once perceived as dark, overdecorated ("too much is not enough" could be the Victorian motto), fussy, and complicated, is now treasured for its variety, craftsmanship, and its reflection of a rich and vibrant age.

Technically, the Victorian era ran from Queen Victoria's ascension to the throne in 1837 until her death in 1901—an exceptionally long run for a single style. Thus Greek, Gothic, Italianate, and Second Empire would all be Victorian, and we don't normally include them here. Nevertheless, Victorian works as a convenient umbrella for a range of substyles that convey the entrepreneurial and rough and tumble spirit of late nineteenth-century America. Victorian allows for all sorts of seemingly indefinite stylistic labels—Victorian Gothic, High Victorian, Franco-Victorian, even Queen Anne. The labeling of architectural styles has become increasingly complicated; a perusal of Downing's *Country Houses* turns up Anglo-Italian, Norman, Southern Villa-Romanesque, to name just a few.

The aim of this guidebook is to simplify rather than to complicate. But it is sometimes impossible to sort out all the varied influences and sources of a style, especially in a time of such explosive change. The nineteenth century was a cataclysmic period: the growth of democracy and nationalism, technology and the transformation of the old agricultural economies, the movement of people to cities and across oceans, not to mention the expansion of empires of a magnitude not seen since Rome.

For America, the Civil War was the defining moment—the final loss of our New World innocence. The time we normally call Victorian coincided with our recovery from the conflict, ushered in by the Centennial celebration in Philadelphia. There was more money to build more houses for more people, and new methods of constructing, selling, and transporting houses. The balloon frame, new saws, new materials, increased publication and distribution of magazines and books—lots of new *everything*—changed the face of architecture, no less on the domestic front.

STICK STYLE

Americans love wood houses. The bargeboards and decorative trim of the Gothic cottage wildly proliferated in the 1850s, 1860s, and 1870s. While new milling techniques, woodworking tools, and mass production made this possible, the decorative impulse was fueled by a demand for greater stylistic choices. But the Stick Style's restless experimental nature was more than fashion. There are major examples designed by the leading architects of the day, but some of the best and most adventurous houses might be labeled vernacular. The Stick Style is unusual, too, in that it is not tied to an historical event or famous person. While visually frivolous at times, there is something no-nonsense about the style.

The Stick Style takes its name from the stick work that outlined most of its component blocks: walls, gable ends, and porch pediments all featured framing. This included diagonal braces, reminiscent of medieval half-timbering, along with a series of flat patterns of vertical and horizontal exposed beams that were often painted in contrasting colors. One of the most distinctive characteristics is bracing that spans the triangular-shaped gable ends created by the deep overhanging eaves.

Some of all this woodiness had its roots in Downing's published cottage designs, notably the Swiss Chalet. Some historians see the bold outlines as reflecting the nineteenth-century preoccupation with truthfulness of construction—that the various members express both framing and the idea of wood. Stick Style also had its roots in such style manuals as *Rural Homes* (1851) by English architect Gervase Wheeler (1815–1872) and *Village and Farm Cottages* (1856) by American architect Henry W.

Cleaveland (1827–1919). As we have seen, Americans have a practical streak, and Stick Style elements were easily reproduced—stock elements from mills, available through catalogues. Some Stick Style houses were prefabricated, transported by ship or rail, and erected miles or states away from the forest and lumber mills.

A Stick Style house, often called a cottage, looked less substantial than, say, a heavy brick house with a mansard roof and tall crested tower. But that was part of the style's charm, and the references to Alpine chalets or mountain retreats suggested leisure and second homes. Stick Style was in vogue along the seaside and in summer watering holes and some bigger name architects such as Americans Richard Morris Hunt (1827–1895) and E. T. Potter (1831–1904) tried their hands at wood vacation houses. But in all iterations, the Stick Style had porches with rather more structural elements than necessary, picturesque skylines, and an abundance of decorative trusses in its numerous gables.

So much of American culture comes with European baggage, and the Stick Style had a strong English accent as well. And at the end of its run, the decorative elements acquired more curves and showed marks of the lathe. These changes echoed the popular furniture books of the English art critic and architect Charles Locke Eastlake (1836–1906). His *Hints on Household Taste* (published in Boston in 1872) gave new life to the basic brackets of the Stick Style, as Eastlake's more vigorous forms were adopted and pushed by American lumber mills. The sticklike delicacy faded further into the past as the profusion of heavier forms seem to blend into the subsequent Queen Anne Style.

GEORGE C. MASON HOUSE, **1874**, Newport, Rhode Island.

GRISWOLD HOUSE, **1862**, Newport, Rhode Island. Richard Morris Hunt, Architect. Stick Style masterpiece by Newport's premier late nineteenth-century architect. / **OPPOSITE: HOUSE**, **ca. 1890**, Chicago, Illinois.

HOUSE, ca. 1887, Los Angeles, California. Stick works well with standard lumber, no doubt shipped from Northern California.

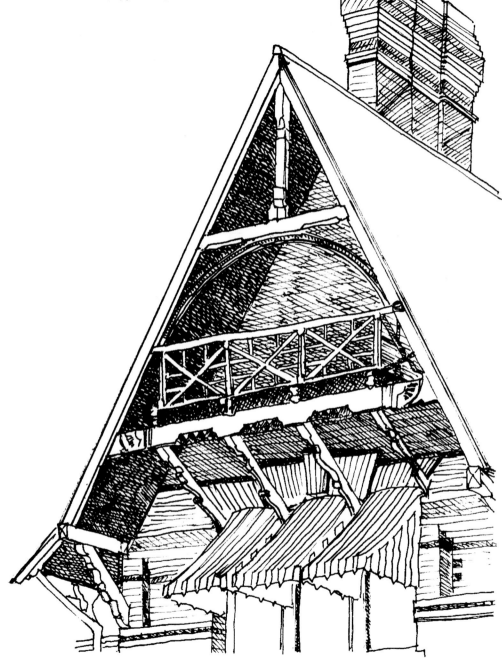

HOUSE, ca. 1890, Chicago, Illinois.

MCKINNEY-MCDONALD HOUSE, ca. 1875, Galveston, Texas. Whimsical Stick Style in a tropical climate.

TANNER HOUSE, **1888**, Portland, Oregon. Standardized lumber in a lumber state.

stick style notes on the defining characteristics

GENERAL PROPORTIONS

Tall and narrow. Emphasis on wood as a material, and linearity.

ROOF TYPES AND FEATURES

From simple gable to very picturesque compositions of projecting eaves, dormers, towers, polygonal turrets, weathervanes, and cast-iron cresting; occasional mansards. Roofs are wide, flaring, quite steep, and generally covered with wood shingles, sometimes decorative slate shingles.

FENESTRATION

Windows range from standard two-over-two to narrower one-over-one, while square single-pane groupings of windows may run along beneath the eaves.

STRUCTURAL AND FACEWORK MATERIALS

Examples are almost always made of wood; the stickwork that outlines the planes of the houses and seemingly arranges them into a series of flat panels is what gives the style its characteristic mien. The wall boards can be horizontal, vertical, fish scale, or a mix. Open trusses and, sometimes, braced arches span the many projecting gables. Scroll-sawn elements contribute to abundant porch braces, railings, and window surrounds.

SPATIAL DESIGNATION AND FLOOR PLAN

No single characteristic plan; usually a rectangular box, but can vary, with L-shaped, cruciform plans, and other asymmetrical possibilities. Use of extended porches and somewhat flowing interior room arrangements shows debt to Italianate.

CHIMNEY PLACEMENT

Chimneys can rise up from the outer walls or along the main roof ridge, but they barely can compete with the finials, towers, and cresting that make up the picturesque skyline of the Stick Style house.

ENTRANCEWAY ATTRIBUTES

Doorways can be placed almost anywhere, but the paneling often reflects the stickwork of the facade.

COLOR

A palette of two or three contrasting colors. Early ones appeared with earth tones—say, light brownstone with darker brown trim, but the appearance of tertiary colors such as olive and terra-cotta enlivened the color combinations.

FAMA HOUSE, ca. 1901, Troy, New York. Front elevation.

QUEEN ANNE

The name Queen Anne reminds us once again that however rebellious and independent Americans might be, we still owe a lot to England for our architectural culture. The eponymous monarch was the last Stuart, and although furniture is associated with her early eighteenth-century reign, she had nothing to do with the wonderfully exuberant style we have come to know as Queen Anne. We are not so much stuck with a curious label as having completely adopted it for one of our most beloved domestic expressions.

As a Victorian-era style, Queen Anne owed much to the Arts and Crafts movement that developed in large part as a reaction to industrialism. Upset by what they saw as the low aesthetic level of the Great Exhibition of 1851 in London (which they blamed on the machine), reformers sought to change the way goods were manufactured. Some forward thinkers attempted to employ new materials and technology to improve the cultural level and economic lot of the workers as well as the objects they produced. Other nostalgic Romantics believed that artisans should return to making everything by hand, to try to recover a time when unknown craftsmen toiled at creating beautiful things. Some artists even re-created medieval guilds and moved to the countryside to produce handmade houses and their furnishings.

The leading handcraft proponent was William Morris (1834–1896). Along with his Pre-Raphaelite friends who revered painting from before the Renaissance, Morris and architect Philip Webb fomented a revolution with the designing and decoration of the Red House (1859), a plain brick dwelling at Bexley Heath, Kent, that recaptured the spirit of the country rather than the grand Neo-Georgian piles and palazzi of the new British merchant class. The social goals of the Arts and Crafts movement were arguably not achieved, but the hand-blocked wallpapers, hand-rushed chairs, and hand-hewn timbered cottages had an enormous and lasting influence. The houses of Scottish architect Richard Norman Shaw (1831–1912) were widely published and became the most important single source for the American Queen Anne.

Most Americans did not care about Morris's social ideals, but we wanted Queen Anne houses here. We loved the illustrations of Shaw's houses in the magazines; we were enchanted by the two British Commissioners houses erected at the Philadelphia Centennial; and we loved the variety of details in both. Queen Anne allowed us to indulge our fantasies and our desire for ever larger, more comfortable houses. Many of the best features of the Italian villa, like open floor plans and wrap-around verandas, evolved further in the Queen Anne. Vestigial towers became big fat round turrets, while wall surfaces supported as many different textures as possible—half-timber, pebble-dash, bricks (especially in elaborate patterns), stone (both rough and smooth), and terra-cotta (cast in interlacing, crests, shields, dates), not to mention the most picturesque skyline imaginable.

Queen Anne suggested leisure, although not Shaw's Scottish Highlands but rather the American seaside. The watering place of Newport, Rhode Island (a seminal town for a number of stylistic developments from the early eighteenth century onward), was the site of the first Queen Anne: the William Watts Sherman House (1874–75; see page 186). Its architect, Louisiana-native Henry Hobson Richardson (1838–1886), borrowed freely from Shaw and his English colleagues. Although later enlarged, this brick, timber, stone, and stucco house has a lot of the features we expect in American Queen Anne: lively silhouette with terra-cotta cresting, asymmetrical fenestration, half-timbering with both brick and stucco infill, and massive and intricate chimneys. The interior had a large open hall from which living spaces flowed. And, in keeping with the Arts and Crafts ideal of cooperative artistic effort, tiles, stained glass, paintings, and carvings by such artists and designers as John La Farge and Louis Comfort Tiffany and architect Stanford White were added.

The style spread westward as far as Seattle, and into urban areas, and is found in great abundance in the streetcar suburbs of cities like Baltimore, Louisville, and St. Louis, and virtually everywhere wealth could support the style's wealth of decoration.

HOUSE, ca. 1884, Cortland, New York. Ground-floor and second-story porches. /
OPPOSITE: ROSSON HOUSE, 1895, Phoenix, Arizona. A. P. Petitt, Architect.

HOUSE, **1889**, San Francisco, California. T. C. Matthews & Son, Architects. San Francisco totally embraced the Queen Anne style.

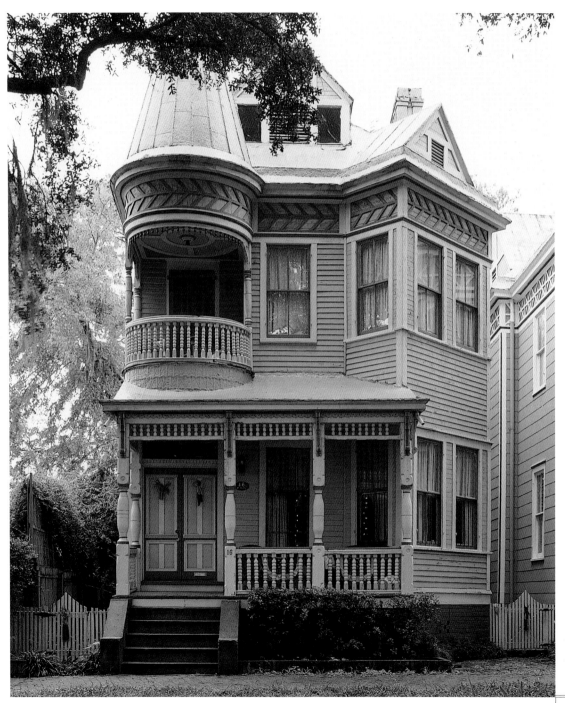

TOWNSEND COTTAGE, ca. 1895, Spring Lake, New Jersey. A veranda for catching sea breezes and watching croquet.

DONNELLY HOUSE, **1893**, Mount Dora, Florida.

HOUSE, ca. 1891, Spring Lake, New Jersey. / **OPPOSITE: PINNEY HOUSE**, 1887, Los Angeles, California.

For the speculative house developer, where does Stick end and Queen Anne begin?

HOUSE, ca. 1888, Spring Lake, New Jersey. How many patterns can be fashioned from millwork?

MARTIN MALONEY HOUSE, **1892**, Spring Lake, New Jersey. Willis G. Hale, Architect. Exuberant Victoriana (note sunburst porch gable) by an important Philadelphia architect.

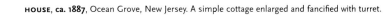

HOUSE, ca. 1887, Ocean Grove, New Jersey. A simple cottage enlarged and fancified with turret.

OPPOSITE: HOUSE, **ca. 1890**, Louisville, Kentucky. Mason Maury, Architect. Maury, an inventive Kentucky designer influenced by Richardson and Sullivan, used brick here for his textured surfaces. / **J. M. EVANS HOUSE**, **1893**, Phoenix, Arizona. Queen Anne in the desert . . . or Queen Anne in the Wild West.

HOUSE, 1892, Minneapolis, Minnesota. Babb, Cook & Willard, Architects. All stone makes for a less lively version of the style. / OPPOSITE: HOUSE, 1890, Seattle, Washington. The wood Queen Anne fits perfectly in the Pacific Northwest.

WILLIAM WATTS SHERMAN HOUSE, **1874–76**, Newport, Rhode Island. H. H. Richardson, Architect. America's first great Arts and Crafts/Queen Anne. / **OPPOSITE: WILLIAM MCKENDRIE CARSON HOUSE**, **1885**, Eureka, California. Ornament detail. Samuel and Joseph Newsom, Architects.

HOUSE, **ca. 1887**, Pasadena, California.

RANKIN-ORELL HOUSE, ca. 1897, Wilmington, North Carolina. An upstairs sleeping
porch is ideal for a sultry seacoast town.

HUTCHINGS, SEALY HOUSE, ca. 1875, Galveston, Texas. George B. Stowe, Architect.

EDGEWOOD, **1886**, Lake Helen, Florida. John Porter Mace, Architect.

JOHN D. FLANNER HOUSE, **ca. 1855**, New Bern, North Carolina.

GENERAL PROPORTIONS

Verticality and complex, picturesque silhouettes.

ROOF TYPES AND FEATURES

One of the most complicated, composed of all sorts of steep slopes, turrets, chimneys, finials, and heavily decorated cornices and bargeboards. Can be shingled with wood or slate, in scalloped or other patterns.

FENESTRATION

May have windows of several different sizes and configurations. While panes of glass became quite large in this period, often only the bottom half of the window has a single pane, while the upper half consists of multi-pane sash, often colored. Window openings can be single rectangles or larger groupings (most often in threes) or even curved, as in wrapped around an oriel.

STRUCTURAL AND FACEWORK MATERIALS

Stone, brick, and wood, often combined: a heavy rusticated stone base, brick first story, frame or shingled upper story. Wooden porches constructed of turned posts and decorated with all manner of scroll-sawn devices. Wall surfaces can have patterns formed by scalloped shingles, recessed bricks, terra-cotta medallions. Gable ends may have elaborate bargeboards.

SPATIAL DESIGNATION AND FLOOR PLAN

Asymmetrical plans reflective of very busy exterior compositions; can have four quite different sides. Houses often hinge around giant staircases that descend into large entrance halls from which flow large, comfortable rooms.

CHIMNEY PLACEMENT

A key visual element of the style, chimneys are tall, brick, ribbed in the Elizabethan manner, and have elaborate caps; they are often placed along the outside walls.

ENTRANCEWAY ATTRIBUTES

Main entrances are often marked by elaborate individual porches or aedicules that echo other vertical elements on the house, such as a tower; porte-cochères are popular, too. Or, less dramatic, the entrance is beneath a broader veranda. The doorways can be just as varied as windows, with single- and multi-pane glazing, paneling, and incised decoration.

COLOR

The variety of materials provides its own color range, but all kinds of dark stains and newly available tertiary colors were applied to wood surfaces and trim in richly complex combinations. For example, body colors of brownstone, amber, and terra-cotta, with gold and bronze and green trim.

BEATH-DICKEY HOUSE, ca. 1898, Atlanta, Georgia. Queen Annes looked good in growing streetcar suburbs.

RICHARDSONIAN

Henry Hobson Richardson was the first person not a European monarch to have an American style named for him; he was also a considerable shaping force in the Queen Anne and Shingle styles. Richardson, too, was the first American architect to have an appreciable influence in Europe, thus reversing the usual east-to-west transatlantic effect. Although little known beyond the realm of architecture, Richardson was a remarkable and towering figure in the late nineteenth-century cultural landscape of the United States.

The second American student at the École des Beaux-Arts in Paris, Richardson soaked up France's architectural legacy, which stretches back to ancient Rome (as we have seen in the Queen Anne, England's patrimony did not go unnoticed by the American student). Through study and travel, Richardson absorbed the most classical of the medieval styles, the Romanesque. The heavily articulated round arches, massive walls, and love of rock-faced masonry became his hallmarks. He initially worked in other styles, too. His first nationally recognized monument, Trinity Church (1872–77) in Boston, was designed in the Victorian Gothic before being transformed into a uniquely Richardsonian masterpiece. His own house on Staten Island, New York, was Second Empire; his William Watts Sherman House in Newport, Rhode Island, helped establish the Queen Anne, yet his most intriguing houses were Shingle Style. Nevertheless, it was Richardson's hugely popular stone churches, public buildings, and houses that supplied the forms emulated in domestic structures all across America.

It was not his own houses but the thousands of copies that made for the style first known as Romanesque Revival, then Richardson Romanesque, and then just Richardsonian. The style was popular everywhere, especially in industrial cities such as St. Louis, Chicago, Louisville, Baltimore, and Cincinnati. Richardsonian adherents borrowed the towers and corner porches from the contemporaneous Queen Anne, but what the public wanted was the round arches, vigorous stonework, and simplified massing so identified with Richardson.

Too often Richardson's admirers failed to understand the master's underlying Beaux-Arts planning principles—he designed from the inside out; his stylistic flourishes were based on an underlying structural logic. Would-be Richardsonians mixed forms and employed details seemingly without understanding the rationale behind them. But none of this seemed to matter to builders and buyers who had to have a solid-looking house made, if possible, of large stones with the characteristic round arches. Richardson died in 1886, and his Romanesque flourished for another decade. But the style faltered without Richardson as a continuing source of inspiration, not to mention the cost of such massive houses, as well as the severe depression of 1893–97.

Richardsonian was employed for country estates, but his style was more often seen in rows of similar houses along boulevards of streetcar suburbs. Here, lines of stone turrets recalling a medieval fortress in the Pyrenees, say, and round-arched windows reminiscent of a pre-Gothic monastery along the pilgrimage road to Santiago de Compostela, and walls strong enough to withstand an attack by Richard the Lion-Hearted's armies, spoke of a bourgeois solidity. When done right, Richardsonian houses appear to have been built for the ages.

GEORGE SEALY MANSION, 1891, Galveston, Texas. McKim, Mead & White, Architects. Architects who apprenticed with Richardson employ the master's characteristic eyebrow windows.

WILLIS-MOODY MANSION, **1895**, Galveston, Texas. Heavy masonry arcades set off by brick and a skyline of turrets.

WLLIAM TEMPLE HOUSE, **1892**, Portland, Oregon. Whidden and Lewis, Architects.
Debts to both Richardson and the English Arts and Crafts. / **DRAWING: PAYNE**
MANSION, **ca. 1890**, Troy, New York. Column detail.

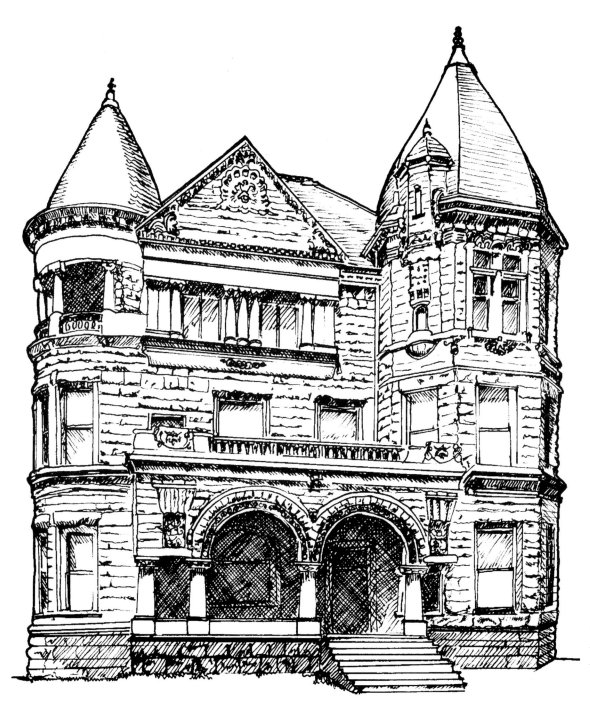

THEOPHILUS CONRAD HOUSE, ca. 1894, Louisville, Kentucky. Front elevation.

HOUSE, ca. 1890, Louisville, Kentucky. Mason Maury, Architect. Louisville has boulevards lined with Richardsonian houses like this. /
OPPOSITE: ANKENY-GOWEY HOUSE, **1891**, Seattle, Washington. Rudolf Ankeny, Architect. A Richardsonian tower, arch, and eyebrow window all in a modest frame house.

DRAWING: A typical window detail. / **GLESSNER HOUSE**, 1886, Chicago, Illinois. H. H. Richardson, Architect. Except for the heavy voussoirs over the doorway, the house is virtually astylar.

LIGHTNER HOUSE, **1896**, St. Paul, Minnesota. Cass Gilbert, Architect. Richardsonian—and early—work by one of America's great neoclassicists.

GENERAL PROPORTIONS

Monolithic, massive forms that have a medieval verticality.

ROOF TYPE AND FEATURES

Usually monochromatic, with large broad masses. The tile, slate, or wood shingles may be topped with ridge tiles and finials and enlivened by corner towers and the characteristic eyebrow dormer, but the overall sense of roof is strong.

FENESTRATION

The arch is the distinguishing mark of the style, although there are windows with heavy flat lintels and stone mullions. Windows tend to get proportionally smaller with each successive story; there are often groups of windows under the main cornice that are comprised of single panes topped with multipane glazing; windows are framed by stubby, short Romanesque engaged columns.

STRUCTURAL AND FACEWORK MATERIALS

Stone, particularly granite and brownstone, often brick, or combinations; heavy, ashlar masonry found on the ground floor and ideally on all stories. Brick used on upper stories, or for the entire facade. Decorative carving throughout.

SPATIAL DESIGNATION AND FLOOR PLAN

While outlines may be blocky, floor plans can be quite open and inventive, although an entrance hall is the central feature from which the other rooms radiate.

CHIMNEY PLACEMENT

Stacked brick or stone chimneys can be freestanding or emerge from parapets and towers.

ENTRANCEWAY

Double doors, reached by crossing the main porch or contained beneath a large, deeply recessed round arch.

COLOR

Masonry, preferably grays and browns, and brick. When employed, roof tiles are red.

CONRAD HOUSE, **1895**, Louisville, Kentucky. Clarke and Loomis, Architects. A veritable catalogue of Richardsonian decorative elements, the house was called "Conrad's Folly."

SHINGLE STYLE

The Shingle Style is one of the most wholly American styles. In contrast to earlier styles, such as Second Empire and Italianate, reflecting the worlds of the Empresses Eugénie and Victoria, the Shingle Style derives its chief inspiration from the humbler fishermen's and farmers' cottages, along with their attendant barns and outbuildings, of America itself, especially New England. The Shingle Style was exclusively domestic. It was also an artistic and aesthetic triumph.

Shingle is a modest material. Throughout the eighteenth century in Rhode Island, for example, a house might have a clapboard face to present to the world, while the sides and back of the house would be shingled. Shingles were less costly to make than clapboards (you didn't need a sawmill), easier to install, and they could be maintained and repaired more simply. When made of certain woods, such as cedar, they required no paint; near the seacoast, where the salt air saturated the wood with a pussy willow softness, the shingles weathered to a handsome patina. It was this no-nonsense, completely unselfconscious approach to building, rather than the high art of architecture that so enthralled young architects from the 1870s through the turn of the twentieth century, that strengthened the appeal of Shingle Style for so many others.

It was the Beaux-Arts-trained Richardson, who, when not working with stone in the Romanesque, created some of the outstanding monuments of shingled construction. Richardson grasped the essentially plastic and malleable qualities of wood shingles; he understood that they were best when not used in imitation of other materials. His Stoughton House (1882–83) in Cambridge, Massachusetts, was essentially *astylar*. More important, the *absence of style* engendered a free spirit that was passed along to modern pioneers both at home and abroad. The plans that echoed the relaxed exteriors also influenced later open planning, such as Frank Lloyd Wright's Prairie Style. The generally recognized masterpiece of the Shingle Style was the William G. Low House (1887) in Bristol, Rhode Island, by McKim, Mead & White. Variously compared to a barn or an airplane wing, the Low House was what it was: a comfortable summer home that took advantage of a site overlooking Narragansett Bay and that paid homage to the regional domestic design.

Other architects, several of whom had studied with Richardson in his Brookline, Massachusetts, atelier, erected Shingle Style "cottages" in watering places along the New England coast, like Boston's North Shore and Mount Desert Island in Maine, as well as in the White Mountains in New Hampshire and the Berkshires in Massachusetts. Some of these got so large, and their patrons demanded more decoration, so that they almost became versions of the Queen Anne in wood. Wonderful as those rambling summer estates could be, it was the more modest versions built for professors and artists in places like Dublin, New Hampshire, and Waterford, Connecticut, that best showed the accomplishment of this indigenous expression.

The Shingle Style was not limited to New England, or even to the Northeast for that matter. Coverage in magazines and journals meant that the style would have adherents in the Rockies and along the California coast, and there were inventive groups of Shingle Style architects in New York, Philadelphia, Chicago, and San Francisco, and everywhere in between. The style also experienced a minor revival in the 1970s and 1980s as part of Post-Modernism's rediscovery of the past.

HOUSE, 1914, San Francisco, California. William C. Hays, Architect. The shingled skin gives the house a look that is both medieval and modern.

HOUSE, ca. 1888, Evanston, Illinois. Enoch Hill Turnock, Architect.

TOP: BUCKINGHAM HOUSE, 1918, Pasadena, California. Sylvanus Marston, Architect. / **BOTTOM: HOUSE, 1910**, San Francisco, California. Bernard Maybeck, Architect. Originating in New England perhaps, but shingles found committed adherents to the malleable material such as Maybeck on the West Coast. / **OPPOSITE: HOUSE, 1892**, San Francisco, California. Samuel Newsom, Architect. Bay Area architects were quite inventive in their use of shingles.

HOUSE, **1890**, St. Paul, Minnesota. Shingle Style owes much to Queen Anne and foreshadows Colonial Revival.

OPPOSITE, TOP: PINEHURST, ca. 1886, Dublin, New Hampshire. Less well known than Newport, Dublin, nestled beneath the slopes of Mount Monadnock, was a literary and artists colony. / **BOTTOM: SANGER HOUSE**, 1882–83, Montauk, New York. McKim, Mead & White, Architects. One of seven houses built as a summer retreat and fishing community—all laid out by Frederick Law Olmsted. / **ISAAC BELL HOUSE**, 1881–83, Newport, Rhode Island. McKim, Mead & White, Architects. Epitome of the Shingle Style: different textures and shapes unified in a large, elegant yet informal-feeling "cottage."

PAGES 218–219: ANGLECOTE, 1893–1910, Philadelphia, Pennsylvania. Wilson Eyre, Architect. More than a summer cottage, a magnificent example of the Shingle Style by the inventive Philadelphia designer.

shingle style notes on the defining characteristics

GENERAL PROPORTIONS

Horizontal, rambling, casual.

ROOF TYPE AND FEATURES

Wood shingles, arrayed in very broad masses. Recalling the Colonial saltbox, asymmetrical roofs may have one pitch that slopes down from the ridge two or more stories and may almost touch the ground; lower slopes of the roofs act as porch roofs. Dormers, towers, chimneys may momentarily break up the broad roof surfaces, but the roof is a key element of the style's composition.

FENESTRATION

Rectangular, double-hung sash, with either mullions (say, eight-over-eight) or multipane top sash over single-pane glazing below. Windows are often grouped in twos or threes.

STRUCTURAL AND FACEWORK MATERIALS

Shingle. These houses are usually built upon stone bases, but they are otherwise thoroughly wood houses. The shingles spread across various vertical and sloped surfaces almost like a skin. Visible structural elements, such as porch posts and cornices, are plain.

SPATIAL DESIGNATION AND FLOOR PLAN

Generally rectangular, although porches, towers, and wings may break up the generally boxlike plans. Like their contemporary Queen Anne and Richardsonian brethren, have substantial entrance halls that act as a staging area for the adjacent spaces—and for the staircase to the upper floors.

CHIMNEY PLACEMENT

Massive chimneys, arrayed along the outside walls, usually brick, although many have stone bases and some are rough masonry throughout.

ENTRANCEWAY

Entrance approached through porch, or the doorway may have its own smaller porch. Entrances are decidedly unmonumental.

COLOR

Wood shingles range from light gray to dark brown, depending upon age and proximity to salt air; if stained, the color is always brown. Wood trim is traditionally dark green or dark red.

SKINNER HOUSE, **1881**, Newport, Rhode Island. Tower facade. McKim, Mead & White, Architects.

08

CLASSICAL REVIVALS: AN OVERVIEW

The turn of the twentieth century marked a major shift in the way Americans perceived and employed history. The United States had changed dramatically. We had experienced a cataclysmic civil war and were assuming the mantle of a world power. The way in which the past was used also changed, from lighthearted and at times naive to a more scholarly approach freighted with import. The Beaux-Arts style, a full-blown European classicism, is rarely whimsical in the way that the application of a few Doric columns to a simple farmhouse had been during the Greek Revival. The very scale of much larger houses in the spirit of Italian Renaissance palaces or English country estates in the manner of Sir Christopher Wren demanded a different mind-set.

One of those rich ironies in which American architecture abounds is that, in reaching deeper and more seriously into the classical and medieval past for inspiration, our houses became more particularly American. We used the past as a starting point and did not let history weigh upon us too heavily. The homes of the putative robber barons by Richard Morris Hunt, McKim, Mead & White, Carrère & Hastings, and other European-trained architecture firms are some of the most exuberant and creative domestic examples to grace this side of the Atlantic. Their followers—a second generation of so-called eclectic designers—continued to produce handsome versions of French, Georgian, and Elizabethan. And following World War I, various period versions would make Tudor and Colonial staples of suburban development from then on.

There was another side to house design in this period: a more modern streak. Because of the pervasive tenets and persuasive teachers of Modernism, entire generations of architecture students were taught to regard the revived styles of the Beaux-Arts and any other historically based fashion as inferior. This vilification and burying of the past by European and then American Modernism transformed the term eclecticism into a derogatory one. Regardless of our opinions about these opposing viewpoints, there is no denying that there was a reaction to academicism.

If only it were all as simple as Beaux-Arts versus Modern. The period was unusually complex, and while we were building the great mansions of Newport, we were also developing the Craftsman bungalow. Frank Lloyd Wright (who jeeringly referred to Beaux-Arts-trained architects as "Bozos") may have overthrown the old order with his Prairie Style, yet his roots were very much in the nineteenth century—with debts to Thomas Jefferson, as well as to the Arts and Crafts movement.

BEAUX-ARTS

Beaux-Arts, although originally a French term, has become thoroughly integrated into American architectural terminology. It refers to the high-style classicism introduced into this country by Parisian-trained Americans like Richard Morris Hunt, John Mervin Carrère (1858–1911), and Charles Follen McKim (1847–1909). Beaux-Arts houses were grand, sometimes pretentious, and often decorated with giant columns and the other trappings of historical styles, particularly Roman.

For many Modernists, however, the very name was anathema and was used pejoratively to put down anyone who believed in the classical canons of taste or relied upon the ancient orders. Opponents of that broad spectrum of classicism that flowered here in the late nineteenth and early twentieth centuries argued against relying on the past for architectural inspiration. Today, Beaux-Arts is accepted as a legitimate expression and not as symbolic of the failure of native creativity.

The École des Beaux-Arts was originally founded by Louis XIV to supply architects and designers to build the palace at Versailles—and to further glorify the "Sun King." Closed during the Revolution, it was reestablished by Napoléon in the early nineteenth century. Architectural training was based upon a thorough understanding of the classical orders, and although the primary emphasis seemed to be appearances rather than structure, students were instructed in a system of rationality and clarity.

There were no American architectural schools until after the Civil War (the Massachusetts Institute of Technology was founded in 1865, the University of Illinois in

1868, and Cornell in 1871), so the ambitious aspiring architects went to Paris to study. Hunt was the first American to do so, followed by Richardson (who despite his Romanesque style never abandoned the École planning principles), and eventually by many others. As American architecture programs opened, they adopted the Beaux-Arts system and ensured the spread of academic classicism.

The grand buildings of the newly imperial America—the World's Columbian Exposition in Chicago in 1893, the New York Pubic Library, the Metropolitan Museum of Art, countless post offices, railroad stations, and state capitols—sprouted up everywhere as giant re-creations of Rome seen through Francophile eyes. Houses, too, kept pace with the style and account for some of the key monuments of the Beaux-Arts.

Beaux-Arts classicism is inextricably associated with a Gilded Age peopled by newly rich entrepreneurs who were in search of a legitimacy that a royal, autocratic style might provide. Astors, Vanderbilts, Morgans, and other fabulously rich families contributed to glamorous, sometimes scandalous, societal tales in châteaux along the seaside, castles in the mountains, and palazzi along New York's Fifth Avenue. Newport, as America's first resort, comes to mind, with Hunt's The Breakers (1892–95; site of a Vanderbilt daughter's wedding to an impoverished English duke) or American architect Horace Trumbauer's (1868–1938) The Elms (1899–1901). As settings for the novels of Edith Wharton and Henry James, they captured the good times of an era before World War I and before the income tax destroyed the old order.

A house such as Hunt's Biltmore (1890–95) in Asheville, North Carolina, a re-creation of an Early Renaissance château worthy of François I, is hardly the norm. But the Beaux-Arts style filtered down to upper-middle-class and middle-class homes, especially along the streetcar suburbs in newly wealthy cities like St. Louis, Chicago, Minneapolis, and Louisville. Whether with just the use of columns, cleverly retrieved details from France and Italy, or gargantuan scale, a good Beaux-Arts house offers presence, symmetry, and a rational, clear plan.

F.W. CARPENTER HOUSE, **1896**, Providence, Rhode Island. Carrère and Hastings, Architects.

Paris' Place des Voges and the style of Louis XIII for a merchant prince.

GRABFELDER HOUSE, ca. 1899, Louisville, Kentucky. W. J. Dodd and Arthur Cobb, Architects. /

OPPOSITE: HOUSE, 1897, Louisville, Kentucky. A cosmopolitan urban house for a grand boulevard.

OPPOSITE, TOP: **HOUSE**, **1918**, Dallas, Texas. Intentionally evoking the White House. / **BOTTOM: HOUSE**, **ca. 1910**, Sea Girt, New Jersey. / **HOUSE**, **ca. 1913**, Birmingham, Alabama. A Doric portico, the grandeur of Rome rather than the simpler Greek style.

DAVID ATKINS HOUSE, **1866**, San Francisco, California. Like a casino from an Italian Renaissance garden of the sixteenth century. Architect Julia Morgan did the renovation in 1915.

CLARENCE AND KATHERINE DUER MACKAY HOUSE, **1899–1902**, Roslyn, New York. Front doorway with Beaux-Arts entablature and surround—probably derived from the doorway at the *Ancien Hôtel de Montescot,* Chartres, France. McKim, Mead & White, Architects.

GENERAL PROPORTIONS

Monumental, formal, invariably symmetrical; theatrical.

ROOF TYPE AND FEATURES

Mansards make a return, especially in urban examples (and have slate shingles and elaborate stone dormers and cornices), but examples often hide their roofs behind classical balustrades.

FENESTRATION

Windows tend to be quite large and are almost always presented with heavy decorative stone surrounds. Windows may be topped by arches, heavy lintels, or bisected by hefty masonry mullions; they can be square, long and narrow (in the Parisian manner), or placed in cruciform frames.

STRUCTURAL AND FACEWORK MATERIALS

The external wall covering of choice is limestone; brick, marble, stucco, and various combinations abound. The exterior facing implies wealth, luxury, and abundance, so quoins, columns, window moldings, and decorative embellishments (such as cartouches, floral wreaths, and putti) are all large and grand. Facades are often enfiladed, layered as if one material was recessed behind another or a window was applied over and in front of the wall.

SPATIAL DESIGNATION AND FLOOR PLAN

Freestanding examples are almost always composed of rectangular masses; these may be expanded in two or three directions (in smaller units as they proceed away from the main block). Floor plans are logical, clear, and rational: typically, a central grand entrance hall bisects the house, with flanking dining and living rooms. The main entrance is the central focus of the house, inside and out.

CHIMNEY PLACEMENT

Chimneys are not usually prominent, and are most often invisible behind classical balustrades. When seen, they are often on the end walls, or paired at each end.

ENTRANCEWAY

The main entrance is almost without exception in the center of the main facade and it is treated accordingly, surrounded by any manner of paired columns, pilasters, archways, and small porches.

COLOR

Sobriety, grandeur, and the appearance of aristocratic forebears is the order of the day, so colors tend to stay within the range provided by the beige limestone, white marble, and red brick.

HYDE HALL (FREDERICK W. VANDERBILT HOUSE), 1895–99, Hyde Park, New York.

Column and entablature detail. McKim, Mead & White, Architects.

GEORGIAN REVIVAL

Georgian Revival recalls both eighteenth-century Colonial America and the Renais-sance forms that inspired the original English Georgian architecture. The initial impulse to revive Georgian forms may have been a nostalgic view backward to a sim-pler era. Charles McKim and Stanford White's (1853–1906) walking tour of New England in the summer of 1877 is often given as the beginning of the interest in American forms. But it was also a return to rationality and classicism that must have seemed attractive after the banquet of Victorian excess—multicolored and multitex-tured surfaces, picturesque skylines, and dark Richardsonian stone. In its reliance upon classical sources and in its clarity of approach, the Georgian Revival parallels the Beaux-Arts.

Style changes can be as fickle as the waistline of an empress's dress. Yet, there was a genuine longing to capture an American spirit, encouraged by the Centennial celebra-tion of 1876. Much of the aesthetic fallout from the great exhibition in Philadelphia was more Victorian, but there was an awakening of national artistic pride. The back-ward look may have been through rose-colored glasses, but the perception of an earlier era exerted a strong pull. When viewed from a world of increasing industrialization and urbanization, not to mention one with a diminishing frontier, 1776 started to look more and more appealing. Eventually, scholarship would catch up with enthusiasm and result in serious projects such as the restoration of Colonial Williamsburg.

In the early stages, there was an English cast to the revival, hence Georgian is far more accurate a label than Colonial. Just as Beaux-Arts-trained architects reached into the treasure chest of forms that comprised the classical traditions of Rome and Paris, often the very same architects turned toward the bounty of England. A wide range of variations was thus available: from the early English Renaissance of Inigo Jones, the "Wrenaissance" of Sir Christopher Wren and his Baroque followers Hawksmoor and Vanbrugh, through the Neo-Palladians of the Burlington Circle, and on to the neoclassicism of Robert Adam. In all its manifestations, Georgian was clearheaded and based on rules; it also provided enough decorative variation to delight even the most fanciful imagination.

Georgian was primarily a domestic style, and so Georgian Revival was a natural for adorning estates of the rich. After the arriviste excesses of, say, a merchant prince's palace at Newport, the Georgian was more like a polite country gentleman visitor—less fun, maybe, but better mannered. The rectangular blocks of warm brick with their symmetrical plans and sensible room-behind-room layouts were a welcome relief after the over-the-top gilded grandeur of the Beaux-Arts. This did not mean that their builders were not just as rich or even nouveau riche. American John Russell Pope (1874–1937), designer of the National Gallery of Art (1937–40), Washington, D.C., Horace Trumbauer, architect of the Philadelphia Museum of Art (1931–38), or Charles A. Platt (1861–1933), creator of the Freer Gallery of Art (1916–21) in Washington, D.C., could just as easily design a country house of red brick, white trim, with a five-part-Palladian country-house plan as an Italian Renaissance villa. They could be just as large.

The revived Georgian also lent itself to smaller houses, especially in the suburbs. Brick walls (or veneered brick walls), the good old double-pile central-hallway plan, and boxlike shapes were easy to replicate. Most of all, Georgian offered a sense of propriety, as well as a certain nationalistic reassurance. Never mind that the source of the decorative detail might be more Wiltshire than New Jersey, Georgian Revival looked right.

TOLESTON HOUSE, **1913**, Pasadena, California. E. P. Zimmerman, Architect. A Swedish or Dutch gambrel for sunny Southern California.

HOUSE, **1916**, Houston, Texas. Warren and Wetmore, Architects. A stately Georgian by the architects of New York's Grand Central Terminal.

OPPOSITE: HOUSE, **1892**, Atlanta, Georgia. Walter Downing, Architect. Adamesque swags and slender columns revived. / **A. V. S. SMITH HOUSE**, **1904**, Jacksonville, Florida. J. H. W. Hawkins, Architect.

HUBBARD-EMORY HOUSE, 1892, Cambridge, Massachusetts.
Longfellow, Alden & Harlow, Architects.

KERSEY COATES REED HOUSE, ca. 1931, Chicago, Illinois. David Adler, Architect.

PARKER HOUSE, **1910**, Seattle, Washington. Frederick Sexton, Architect. The paired columns clearly announce the entrance to the house, while expressing a debt to classical Rome.

BUEHNER HOUSE, **1906**, Portland, Oregon. Whidden and Lewis, Architects. "Tara's Theme" played in the Pacific Northwest.

HOUSE, ca. 1900, Waterford, New York. Dormer detail. / OPPOSITE, TOP: NATHAN AND LILLIAN BARTON HOUSE, 1897, Providence, Rhode Island. Martin and Hall, Architects. / BOTTOM: LEE HOUSE, 1899, Raleigh, North Carolina.

E. R. RICHARDSON HOUSE, **1903**, Houston, Texas. Undoubtedly larger than its Middle Georgian sources, the tetrastyle portico could be borrowed from a Roman temple.

RICHARDSON HOUSE II, 1913, Houston, Texas. Slightly more modest than its predecessor; the fanlight and slender columns suggest Late Roman (and Late Georgian) inspiration.

ANDREWS-LONDON HOUSE, 1918, Raleigh, North Carolina. James. A. Alter, Architect.

An enlarged and perfected version of a Middle Georgian house in Philadelphia.

SKYFIELD, ca. 1913, Harrisville, New Hampshire. Lois Lilly Howe, Architect. Lois Howe was a founder and principal of Howe, Manning & Almy—the first women's architectural firm.

GENERAL PROPORTIONS

Mostly symmetrical, horizontal masses of two to two-and-a-half stories.

ROOF TYPES AND FEATURES

Again, the sources are key here, and while various gambrel shapes are popular, the prototypical roof is the hipped gable of seventeenth- and eighteenth-century England.

FENESTRATION

Double-hung sash, usually six-over-six; also the Palladian window is employed prominently, especially over the main entrance. Simpler versions of the style employ shutters.

STRUCTURAL AND FACEWORK MATERIALS

Mostly brick and frame. Whether masonry or clapboard, they often have pilasters and quoins—usually wood—but sometimes of limestone; limestone is used for swags, garlands, inset panels, medallions and other decorative devices on especially high-style examples.

SPATIAL DESIGNATION AND FLOOR PLAN

While not rigidly symmetrical, a central entrance hall with rooms arrayed on either side is typical. Plans often imitate those of the sources, and so five-part country houses appear, but interior arrangements are more informal. Mass is mitigated by the use of projecting wings or recessed elements, such as an entrance terrace. Circular, elliptical, or oval rooms from Late Georgian are revived, as is the projecting central pavilion of Middle Georgian.

CHIMNEY PLACEMENT

Typically straightforward, tall brick stacks.

ENTRANCEWAY

Front door treatment is typically the major stylistic focus. The doorway itself may have a transom, elliptical fanlight, or sidelights, as well as a heavy entablature or pediment; the aedicule surrounding the doorway is a somewhat scholarly rendition of Georgian doorways from the past: pilasters, columns, and pedimented or balustrated porches.

COLOR

For the non-masonry houses, white dominates, with multi-colored schemes composed of tertiary colors. If not white, then light gray or yellow, or other neutral tints with white trim.

CHARLES CALDER HOUSE, **1896**, Providence, Rhode Island. What appears at first to be a modest cottage is actually a large, formal house with alternating dormer pediments.

craftsman style

THE YEARNINGS OF THE CRAFTSMAN STYLE REPRESENT the opposite of the classical revivals. Beaux-Arts may have emulated the homes of the rich and titled, but the Craftsman house was a workman's bungalow. Instead of grandeur, most Craftsman houses were one and a half stories, with comfortable porches supported by blocky piers—not Corinthian columns. The emphasis was on humble materials—construction joints were proudly exposed—and there was an overwhelming sense of the handmade.

The Craftsman movement may be seen as a byproduct of the national soul-searching that accompanied the Centennial of 1876. The centerpiece of the exposition in Philadelphia was the giant Corliss steam engine, surrounded by the latest manufactured goods. That symbolic image of industrial power obscured a feeling of unease at the loss of the landscape—the despoliation of the Garden of Eden that brought so many people to our shores in the first place.

The desire to emulate a simpler time had been institutionalized by the Arts and Crafts movement in England, and it was winning converts in America. The Rhode Island School of Design was founded in 1877 by Providence ladies who had visited the Centennial, been impressed by the British exhibits, and vowed to establish Arts and Crafts training here. Another influential exhibit in Philadelphia was that of the Shakers. We may think of Shakers as precursors to contemporary design, while they saw themselves as businesspeople supporting their utopian society. The impact of their sparse furniture and household goods must have struck a responsive chord in the hearts of people depressed by all the factory-made items awash with superfluous ornament.

Another influence was not from Europe at all, but from East Asia, particularly Japan. *Japanisme* and Orientalism had appeared in Western painting, but a certain craft aesthetic attracted English and American Arts and Crafts adherents. The entire world of the East was available, as suggested by the Hindi-based word *bungalow*, meaning shelter. A California house, such as the Gamble House by the brothers Charles and Henry Greene in Pasadena, shows an attention to detail that is both

William Morris and Japanese. The constructional elements are articulated with the respect and sensibility of a hand-made Japanese temple.

Arts and Crafts colonies were established on both coasts, but the most famous was Gustav Stickley's Craftsman Farms in northern New Jersey. The main building there drew inspiration from the Colonial homesteads of the area, while its interior had walls of peeled logs. Stickley produced a monthly magazine called *The Craftsman*, which featured homes and all the furniture and decoration that went in them. One contributor, Harvey Ellis, supplied five house designs, including "How to Build a Bungalow" in the December 1903 issue. Stickley's crusading inspired many like-minded villages, such as nearby Mountain Lakes, New Jersey, and the Roycrofters in East Aurora, New York.

Despite the unique handcraft aspect of the style, its popularity led to a broad range of imitations that dispensed with hand-built beams and hand-carved posts. By the end of World War I, prefabricated and mass-produced bungalows, done mostly in the Craftsman style, were available from firms such as Aladdin Company and Sears, Roebuck and Company. The cozy-looking, human-scaled bungalow became a staple of suburban development for decades. Its popularity, as with Craftsman Style, has not diminished.

LEDYARD HOUSE "IDYLLWILD," 1909, Pasadena, California. Craftsman may have grown out of the English Arts and Crafts movement, but California architects developed the style into something both traditional and modern—and not a little Eastern.

CRAFTSMAN STYLE BUNGALOW, ca. 1917. Design 11637-A from *The Cameron & Hawn Book of Homes* by Cameron & Hawn Lumber, Doors, and Trim of Albany, New York.

PAGES 262–263: GAMBLE HOUSE, 1908, Pasadena, California. Greene and Greene, Architects. One of the great American houses: craftsmanship seemingly melding Midwestern, English, and Eastern sensibilities.

HOUSE, ca. 1912, Palm Beach, Florida.

HOUSE, ca. 1910, Pasadena, California. The Greene Brothers perfected the strong overhangs, exposed rafters, and trabeated tectonics that are the distinguishing characteristics of this Pasadena house.

HOUSE, ca. 1915, Tucson, Arizona. A rather large house composed of modest smaller elements.

BURLINGAME HOUSE, ca. 1908, Houston, Texas. George L. Burlingame, Architect. The bungalow became the workingman's Craftsman house.

RHODES HOUSE, **1906**, Pasadena, California. W. J. Saunders, Architect. Sometimes the craft aesthetic can appear as much Swiss chalet as English cottage.

HOUSE, ca. 1910, Phoenix, Arizona. Massive piers, deep porch, and low roof provide an overwhelming sense of shelter.

HOUSE, 1902, Chicago, Illinois. Craftsman certainly overlapped chronologically and literally with Wright's Prairie Style, especially in Chicago.

GILBERT HOUSE, ca. 1890, St. Paul, Minnesota. Variety of wall treatments and surfaces, carved posts, and the wee inglenook window contribute a cozy English-cottage quality.

HOUSE, **1902**, Chicago, Illinois. An asymmetrical approach to the Craftsman house; note trellis treatment above the entrance.

ADELBERT FISCHER HOUSE, **1909**, Philadelphia, Pennsylvania. Milton Medary, Architect. Stucco surfaces, a Chinese-looking roof dormer, and exposed rafter ends contribute to a restrained East Coast version of Craftsman. / **DRAWING: BLACKER HOUSE**, **1907**, Pasadena, California. Craftsman exterior lamp detail. Greene and Greene, Architects.

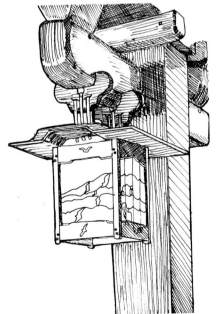

AINSWORTH HOUSE, **1907–18**, Portland, Oregon. William C. Knighton, Architect.

A little bit of nineteenth-century England in a similarly rainy climate.

WILBUR REID HOUSE, **1914**, Portland, Oregon. Francis Brown, Architect. The entire house seems almost hand hewn, with its wall of random boulders and massive English medieval barn-like porch beams.

STIMSON GREEN MANSION, 1901, Seattle, Washington. Kirtland Cutter, Architect. Half-timbering, with an entrance porch that could be the lych gate from an English rural church of the Middle Ages.

ROOS HOUSE, **1909**, San Francisco, California. Bernard Maybeck, Architect. Maybeck was able to fashion English half-timbering into something quite individual, like this unprecedented wall treatment with its almost anthropomorphic carved beams.

WADSWORTH HOUSE, **1925**, Pasadena, California. What could be more handmade, more woodsy, or more expressive of Craftsman construction than a log house?

GENERAL PROPORTIONS

Low-slung, one to one-and-a-half story, cottage-like.

ROOF TYPES AND FEATURES

Often low-pitched, usually gabled (with the gable end perpendicular to the street), and with prominent, overhanging eaves. In bungalow variants, the roof may be of steeper pitch, sometimes double-pitched, but always with roof forming protective front porch. Second story often consists of a single dormer.

FENESTRATION

Double-hung sash, sometimes with smaller multi-pane upper half. Dormer windows may be arranged in groups.

STRUCTURAL AND FACEWORK MATERIALS

Built on fieldstone bases (and with fieldstone chimneys), classic examples are wood, while bungalow variants are frame and often brick. Common are heavy porches supported by chunky square columns and extended eaves with prominent and decorative rafter details. There can be an overemphasis on structural details, such as hinges, pegs, and joints. ·

SPATIAL DESIGNATION AND FLOOR PLAN

Elaborate examples exist, but the basic bungalow, the most common type exhibiting the style, is usually rectangular (with the short side to the street) and rarely have hallways, as the rooms line up one behind the other. A front porch is ubiquitous.

CHIMNEY PLACEMENT

Single chimneystacks, which only rarely are important design elements.

ENTRANCEWAY

Central doorways feature glass in upper third, and often there are wide sidelights.

COLOR

Reflecting the Arts and Crafts movement's emphasis on natural materials, colors tend toward ochres, browns, and muted earth tones, as well as William Morris's favorites of olive and muted terra-cotta reds.

BATCHELDER HOUSE, 1909, Pasadena, California. Ernest Batchelder, Architect.

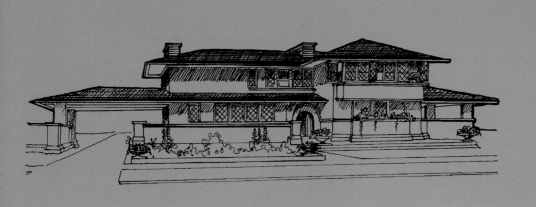

"A SMALL HOUSE IN A PRAIRIE TOWN" was the title of an article in the *Ladies Home Journal* in 1901; it showed a sample house with plans by Chicago architect Frank Lloyd Wright. The house in the prairie town became the Prairie Style and the name stuck. Wright wanted nothing more than to create an entirely new American style, one that would reflect neither Europe nor the past, but the broad expanses of the Midwest. And his houses of the turn-of-the-twentieth century were revolutionary.

Composed of strong horizontal planes that echoed the flat plains of Illinois, his houses were also anchored firmly to the land by large, massive central chimneys, low-pitched roofs with broad overhangs that seemed to hug the ground. Long strips of windows and the use of windows at the corners blur the distinction between inside and outside. Thus, the Prairie house carried within it two characteristic national traits: the restless American spirit—the kind that abandoned the Old World to come and turn the prairie into farmland, and a sense of rootedness, hearth, and home.

Wright (1867–1959) was more than just the initiator of the Prairie Style, in that he became the most influential architect of the Modern period, evolving through several Wrightian styles and creating more than 500 buildings. But Wright's house designs were the most important. He lived until ninety-one, but had he died at, say, fifty, his suburban Chicago houses, among them the William G. Fricke House (1901–02), Ward M. Willits House (1901–02), and Frederick C. Robie House (1906–09), would have still been watersheds of a new domestic age. Claims from the architect himself notwithstanding, it would be naive to believe that Wright's genius was totally self-generating. Richardson and the Shingle Style, as well as Morris and the Arts and Crafts movement, were ancestors of his house designs. The sense of enclosure coupled with the openness of the flowing plans, and the variety of sources, may have been inspired by the past, but Wright brought all of these ideas together in a new way. (Wright also designed everything that went into his houses, from furniture to placemats, from light fixtures to stained glass, from murals to dishes).

Wright's great legacy was the breaking up of the box—the square room-behind-a-room plan we have seen since Colonial times—and replacing it with flowing space. He continued to develop this spatial concept through his inexpensively built Usonian houses during the Great Depression era and in such masterpieces as the incomparable Fallingwater (1935–39) in Mill Run, Pennsylvania. Although Wright designed hundreds of houses, many of which could be interpreted by others as being representative of a particular style, to Wright all were examples of *organic architecture*—a term he conceived to represent, in essence, buildings designed to unite harmoniously with their particular sites (nature) and that are inherently respectful of the human scale. Addressing the subject of style in his 1957 book *A Testament*, Wright wrote, "There is no such thing as true style not indigenous. . . . style only becomes significant and impressive in architecture when it is thus integral or organic."

Wright had apprentices and followers who built their own versions of Prairie Style homes throughout the country. He also had imitators whose thinly veiled copies aped the visual cues of the style without always understanding Wright's principles. Prairie houses appeared in the suburbs and in the house catalogues. The post–World War II Ranch house and the subsequent split-level are direct descendants of the Prairie Style.

The Prairie house was immensely influential in Europe, where Wright's work was extensively published. As a result, many of Wright's revolutionary domestic ideas would be transformed and pushed to the limits by young Modernists who would eventually immigrate to this country and challenge Wright's supremacy.

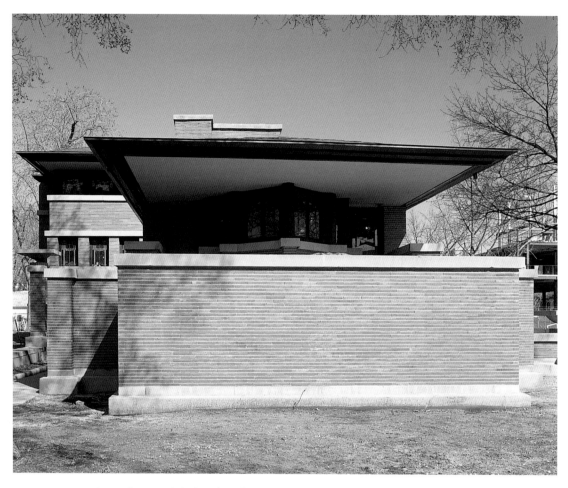

ROBIE HOUSE, 1909, Chicago, Illinois. Frank Lloyd Wright, Architect. The epitome of the Prairie Style, this in-town house offered a massive anchoring chimney, sheltering roofs that echoed the flat landscape, and strips of windows that seemed to dissolve the walls. / **OPPOSITE, TOP: HOUSE, ca. 1910**, Jacksonville, Florida. Wilbur Bacon Camp, Architect. / **BOTTOM: CUMMINGS HOUSE, ca. 1920**, Houston, Texas.

"**A HOME IN A PRAIRIE TOWN**," a design by Frank Lloyd Wright for *Ladies Home Journal*, 1900.

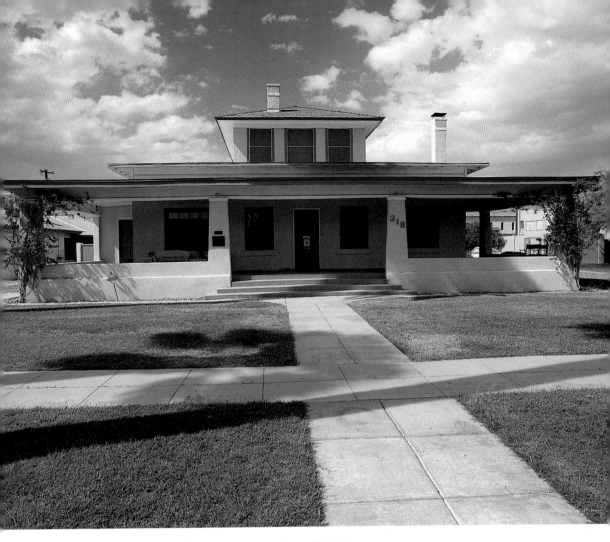

ALKIRE HOUSE, **1911**, Phoenix, Arizona. Franklin Alkire, Architect. Echoes of the Midwestern grasslands in the Arizona desert, with porches that mean business.

WEBER HOUSE, 1921, Los Angeles, California. Lloyd Wright, Architect. A Prairie house by the architect-son of the style's creator. / **OPPOSITE, TOP: BRAY-VALENZUELA HOUSE**, **1917**, Tucson, Arizona. William Bray, Architect. / **BOTTOM: GREMILLION HOUSE**, **1950**, Houston, Texas. Irving Klein, Architect.

H.C. FRENCH, JR., HOUSE, 1910, Pasadena, California. Sylvanus Marston, Architect.

Horizontal strips of narrow casement windows beneath low protective roofs.

HENRY JOHN KLUTHO HOUSE, ca. 1908–25, Jacksonville, Florida. Henry John Klutho, Architect. Two-story window treatment is borrowed from early Wright examples such as the widely published Ward Willits House of 1901.

OPPOSITE, TOP: **THURSTON ROBERTS HOUSE, ca. 1910**, Jacksonville, Florida. Wilbur Bacon Camp, Architect. / **BOTTOM:**
HAYWOOD HOUSE, 1916, Raleigh, North Carolina. / **HOUSE**, 1915, Seattle, Washington. Andrew Willatsen, Architect.
Although not hugging the ground, and raised up to take in the view, echoes of Wright's Chicago houses are strong.

WALSER HOUSE, 1903, Chicago, Illinois. Frank Lloyd Wright, Architect. Wright's use of stucco and wood is clearly articulated here; second-story windows compose an unbroken strip; two ground-floor wings appear to run straight through the house.

HOYT HOUSE, 1913, Redwing, Minnesota. Purcell, Feick & Elmslie, Architects. A house by Wright protégés, with the outlined second story, suggests shoji panels of a traditional Japanese house.

DARWIN MARTIN HOUSE, 1904, Buffalo, New York. Front entry planter detail. Frank Lloyd Wright, Architect. /
OPPOSITE: BLACK HOUSE, 1914, Seattle, Washington. Andrew Willatsen, Architect. The strip of windows
underneath the low horizontal roof pays homage to Wright.

prairie style notes on the defining characteristics

GENERAL PROPORTIONS

Overwhelming sense of horizontality. Asymmetrical building blocks arranged outward rather than upward.

ROOF TYPES AND FEATURES

Roofs are dominating feature and extend way beyond walls to create shelter and shadows; ground-floor rooflines continue from one side of the house to the other. Roofs, usually hipped, have very low pitches.

FENESTRATION

Most examples have casement windows, often arranged in strips, sometimes displacing an entire wall. The panes can be quite small and some have leaded or stained glass.

STRUCTURAL AND FACEWORK MATERIALS

Some examples have wood stickwork or banding that outlines stuccoed walls, although brick is more common—but smooth bricks of a longer dimension to emphasize horizontality. Combinations of plaster and masonry do exist.

SPATIAL DESIGNATION AND FLOOR PLAN

Rooms flow from one to the other; no axes in traditional sense, no doors. Plans radiate outward from central hearth. No attics or basements; houses rarely taller than two stories. Extended overhanging roofs, strips of windows, and low massing blur the line between indoors and outdoors.

CHIMNEY PLACEMENT

A massive chimney in classic examples of the style anchors the house to the land; located near the center of the house, the chimney may serve several fireplaces.

ENTRANCEWAY

As the style percolated down, doorways could be in the front, but in best examples, the entrance rarely fronts the street facade, and is often hard to find, usually on the side under a porte-cochère or reached through a slightly circuitous journey across a terrace or behind a protective wall.

COLOR

Stucco surfaces of neutral colors, such as tan or off-white, while bricks are red, yellow, or tan.

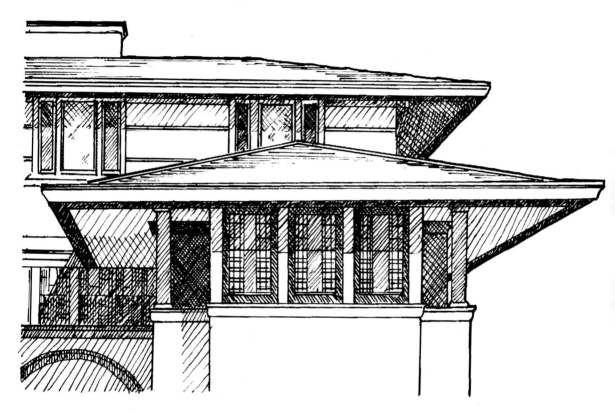

FRANK WRIGHT THOMAS HOUSE, 1901, Oak Park, Illinois. Front facade detail. Frank Lloyd Wright, Architect.

THE END OF WORLD WAR I AND THE BEGINNING OF THE 1920S marked a boom in the proliferation of domestic styles. The grand houses built in the Beaux-Arts style for plutocrats and their Georgian Revival brethren were superseded by a middle-class penchant for suburban dwellings; this trickled down to the working classes as well. The revolutionary developments of Frank Lloyd Wright were of little importance to homebuilders who were lining the leafy boulevards and former farmlands with new homes. The underlying reasons for choosing a style were "Does it look good?" and "What does it say about the house's occupants?"

World War I marked a turning point for civilization—and for Americans because of our role in winning it. President Warren Harding assured us of smooth sailing, while streetcar lines and interurban trains made it possible to build outside of cities. These new suburbs were popular but challenged our notions of community. Whole villages and towns cropped up in places where there was no industry, no commercial center, and no municipality other than an address to identify the collection of homes where city workers retired to mow their lawns and sleep. The houses built then and over the subsequent decades were not high style, but representative of a basic idea of what an American house should look like.

Tudor, Colonial, Dutch Colonial, Spanish Colonial, and dozens of variations in between were there for the borrowing. Oftentimes a developer would use an identical floor plan for a series of houses, but the facade of each would then be decorated in such a way as to suggest different takes on the past—say, stucco and red tile roofs for Spanish Colonial, half-timbering for Tudor, or the addition of window shutters with a heart-shaped motif to suggest Early American. Certain events contributed to a style's popularity, such as the Panama-California Exposition in San Diego in 1915, wherein American architects such as Bertram Grosvenor Goodhue (1869–1924) and Irving Gill (1870–1936) offered their versions of California's glorious Spanish heritage.

Similarly, the strong interest in America's colonial past, gaining ground since 1876, got another boost with the Sesqui-Centennial of 1926. Henry Ford's creation of

Greenfield Village, Michigan, with a copy of Independence Hall as its centerpiece, not to mention the wildly successful restoration of Colonial Williamsburg, meant that porticos, pedimented dormers, and Palladian windows proliferated. The interest was in the theme, not in correct details (never mind that the Colonial Williamsburg restoration destroyed dozens of early buildings that did not suit the image of what its re-creators thought the Virginia capital ought to have looked like in 1742). New homebuyers wanted houses that were easy on the eye, and if they happened to confirm one's national pride, so much the better. (There is a certain irony in the development of historic preservation in the early twentieth century, as various "colonial societies" were established to preserve Yankee or Southern culture, yet the newcomers wanted Colonial just as much as their neighbors.)

It is easy to smile at a stylistic label like Stockbroker's Tudor, or Pueblo, or French Colonial—and the Modernists scoffed at such quaintness, yet these affordable styles answered both desires and demands.

OPPOSITE: **HOUSE, 1908**, San Francisco, California. A. A. Canton, Architect. Mission Revival. The Spanish Baroque window in the gable seems directly inspired by the Mission church at Carmel. / **HOUSE, ca. 1935**, Tucson, Arizona. Mission Revival.

LUNKENHEIMER HOUSE, 1906, Oak Knoll, California. Joseph J. Blick, Architect. Mission Revival. / OPPOSITE, TOP: DODSON-ESQUIVEL HOUSE, ca. 1921, Tucson, Arizona. James Dodson, Architect. Mission Revival. / BOTTOM: CORBETT HOUSE, 1907, Tucson, Arizona. David Holmes, Architect. Mission Revival.

OPPOSITE, TOP: IOANNES HOUSE, **1911**, Oak Knoll, California. Louis B. Easton, Architect. Mission Revival. / **BOTTOM: BILTIMORE HOUSE**, **1911**, Pasadena, California. Irving Gill, Architect. Mission Revival/Modern. Wright pupil Gill borrowed from the spirit of Spanish Colonial to create his own modern aesthetic. / **CAMPBELL HOUSE**, **1924**, Pasadena, California. Roland E. Coate, Architect. Spanish Colonial Revival. Stucco and red tile homes along the Mediterranean Sea are the direct ancestors the Campbell House.

PRINDLE HOUSE, 1926–28, Oak Knoll, California. George Washington Smith, Architect. Spanish Colonial Revival. Memories of Granada from the age of the Moorish rule; maybe inspired by a private wing of the Alhambra. / **OPPOSITE, TOP: GRIFFITH HOUSE, 1924**, Oak Knoll, California. Johnson, Kaufman & Coate, Architects. Spanish Colonial Revival. / **BOTTOM: GABRELLA MANOR, 1938**, Birmingham, Alabama. Spanish Colonial Revival. Inventive Spanish Mission with chapel-like stained-glass window.

OPPOSITE, TOP: EDWARDS HOUSE, ca. 1925, San Marino, California. Roland E. Coate, Architect. Spanish Colonial Revival. Now known as Casa Ru, it evokes a courtyard house in Andalusia from the time of the Moors. / **BOTTOM: UP DE GRAFF HOUSE, 1927**, San Marino, California. Wallace Neff, Architect. Spanish Colonial Revival. / **HOUSE, 1931**, Coconut Grove, Florida. Spanish Colonial Revival.

OPPOSITE, TOP: **HOUSE, ca. 1941**, San Marino, California. Whitney R. Smith, Architect. Monterey Revival. / **BOTTOM:** **VOLK HOUSE, 1940**, Dallas, Texas. Gayden Thomson, Architect. Monterey Revival. / **HOUSE, 1950**, Palm Beach, Florida. Monterey Revival.

HOUSE, ca. 1900, Chicago, Illinois. Tudor Revival. Modest speculative house in "Stockbroker's Tudor." / **OPPOSITE, TOP: HOUSE, 1929**, Houston, Texas. Briscoe and Dixon, Architects. Tudor Revival. One might easily mistake this for a late nineteenth-century manor in the London suburbs. / **BOTTOM: ROTHMAN HOUSE, 1926**, Los Angeles, California. Paul R. Williams, Architect. Tudor Revival. An architecturally convincing Elizabeth manor house not far from Hollywood by one of America's most esteemed African American architects.

HOUSE, ca. 1915, Los Angeles, California. Tudor Revival. / **OPPOSITE, TOP: HOUSE**, 1917–21, Atlanta, Georgia. Henry Hornbostel, Architect. Tudor Revival. An English Tudor manor house by one of the great eclectic designers of the early twentieth century. / **BOTTOM: OSCAR STRAUSS HOUSE**, 1917, Atlanta, Georgia. Hentz, Reid & Adler, Architects. Tudor Revival. The masters of the suburban Atlanta Georgian house were equally adept at handling Tudor.

OPPOSITE, TOP: **MEWBORNE-SUTHERLAND HOUSE**, **1929**, Birmingham, Alabama. Tudor Revival. This could almost be a Colonial Revival house but for the addition of half-timbering in the gables. / **BOTTOM: SHUFORD HOUSE**, **1931**, Wilmington, North Carolina. Hobart Upjohn, Architect. Tudor Revival. Convincingly English Arts and Crafts house by the grandson of Richard Upjohn, leading ecclesiastical architect of the nineteenth century and a contributor of houses to the guidebooks of A. J. Downing. / **HOUSE**, **1920–30**, Troy, New York. Front facade detail.

OPPOSITE, TOP: **STAATS HOUSE**, **1924**, Pasadena, California. Marston, Van Pelt & Maybury, Architects. French Manor. A taste of rural France. / **BOTTOM: GOODWIN HOUSE**, **1930**, Dallas, Texas. Hal Thompson, Architect. French Manor. / **GREESON HOUSE**, **1978**, Baton Rouge, Louisiana. A. Hays Town, Architect. French Colonial Revival. A new house based on the French Colonial River Road plantations (such as Parlange, 1750, and Homeplace Plantation, 1801).

OPPOSITE, TOP: **HOUSE**, **ca. 1920**, Deal, New Jersey. Mediterranean Revival. / **OPPOSITE, BOTTOM: HOUSE**, **ca. 1918**, Dallas, Texas. Anton Korn, Architect. Mediterranean Revival. / **HOUSE**, **1925**, Palm Beach, Florida. Mediterranean Revival.

OPPOSITE, TOP: **LUXEMBURGER HOUSE**, **1922**, Atlanta, Georgia. Hentz, Reid & Adler, Architects. English Colonial Revival. A convincing evocation of a Maryland or Virginia house of ca. 1770. / **BOTTOM: HOUSE**, **1935**, Houston, Texas. Salisbury and McHale, Architects. Neo-Adamesque. Flat pilasters and delicate window fans hark back to 1815 Philadelphia or Boston. / **DUTCH COLONIAL HOUSE** from a **ca. 1917** edition of *The Cameron & Hawn Book of Homes* by Cameron & Hawn Lumber, Doors, and Trim of Albany, New York.

MARTIN HOUSE, ca 1964, Atlanta, Georgia. James Means, Architect. Colonial Revival. An almost line-for-line recreation of an early Georgian Virginia Tidewater house.

99

OPPOSITE, TOP: HOUSE, **1927**, Houston, Texas. Drink Milner, Architect. Colonial Revival. Suburban house making references to George Washington's Mount Vernon. / **BOTTOM: HOUSE**, **1935**, Houston, Texas. Salisbury and McHale, Architects. Colonial Revival. / **HILL, BLOSSOM HOUSE**, **1950**, Wilmington, North Carolina. Colonial Revival. The Cape Cod emerges as a standard and popular suburban house form.

TOP: **ROBERT ALSTON HOUSE**, **1923**, Atlanta, Georgia. Hentz, Reid & Adler, Architects. Colonial Revival. An imposing Early Georgian central block flanked by Middle Georgian temples. / **BOTTOM: CODIGA HOUSE**, **1924**, Pasadena, California. Roland E. Coate, Architect. Regency. / **OPPOSITE: BAKER HOUSE**, **1926**, Wilmington, North Carolina. Colonial Revival. What real estate brochures would refer to as a "center hall Colonial," is a handsomely proportioned eighteenth-century-inspired Georgian.

period styles notes on the defining characteristics

GENERAL PROPORTIONS

There are many variants of the Period house, but generally rectangular boxes of one-and-a-half to two stories tall.

ROOF TYPES AND FEATURES

Gable roofs with dormers for Georgian; saltboxes for Colonial; gambrels for Dutch; mansards for French; nearly flat tiled roof for Spanish; and taller, perhaps multi-peaked for Tudor.

FENESTRATION

Windows pretty much depend upon chosen style: Colonial can have small casements with many small panes; Georgian, the six-over-six double-hung sash, as does much of the Spanish; French, tall and narrow "French" windows; and Dutch Colonials invariably have shutters.

STRUCTURAL AND FACEWORK MATERIALS

Balloon frames with veneers of clapboard, brick, stucco, half-timber, and stone as appropriate to the style chosen.

SPATIAL DESIGNATION AND FLOOR PLAN

Basic unit is rectangular, but it spreads out depending upon the particular stylistic source. Central hallway floor plans, as in the English, French, and Dutch Colonials, predominate; Spanish and Tudor plans may be a little more fluid.

CHIMNEY PLACEMENT

With the exception of the Tudor, chimneys are not major visual elements. Colonial houses ought to have large central chimneys.

ENTRANCEWAY

Dutch houses may have the double "Dutch doors," Tudor doors may have heavy-looking hardware and nails, and there may be metal grille work over doors and windows in the Spanish.

COLOR

White predominates with Colonial-Georgian frame versions, including the Dutch. Tudor houses are usually white and buff, with brown or black framing. Stucco examples in whites, tans, or pastels.

HAMILTON HOUSE, ca. 1924, Pasadena, California. Marston, Van Pelt & Maybury, Architects.
Colonial Revival. *Philadelphia Georgian* describes it more accurately.

12

modern

american deco

international style

modern

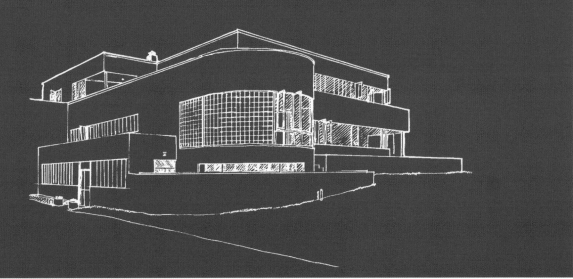

MODERN: AN OVERVIEW

Modern is one of those terms that has been so overused that it is almost useless. Modern means everything new, or, depending upon which historian is speaking, it refers to the current historical epoch that began in the Renaissance, 1750, 1850, or 1950. Even if not the most user-friendly term, however, it remains unavoidable.

For our purposes, Modern refers to those domestic styles that do not—or do not claim—to reply upon past styles. Modern is the style of newness, born of a desire to throw off the past, to begin with a clean slate for a range of societal, political, and aesthetic reasons. Emerging from the ashes of the first World War, Modernism (despite its well-documented roots in the eighteenth and nineteenth centuries) carries with it the promise to toss aside the unimaginative eclecticism of the Beaux-Arts, the Queen Anne, and all the other revivals, and to employ architecture to improve society and make the world a better place in which to live.

Even if a new architectural style could reform society, Modernism turned out not to be monolithic, unchallengeable, or unassailably correct. Within only a few decades of publishing its manifestos and constructing its major monuments, architects and critics were calling for the redeployment of ornament and references to the past. Besides, there was a part of Modernism that never abandoned decoration: Art Deco.

To those taught by Modernists, Modernism seemed to be the *only* style, as well as the only system of architectural ethics. Professors at some of the most influential design schools railed against borrowing from the past, argued that the 1893 World's Columbian Exposition in Chicago set back American architecture half a century. They gravely pontificated with the certain knowledge of the true believer that American houses needed to be *honest*, which meant factory sash, flat roofs, and not a hint of the Colonial anywhere. That a majority of housebuilders and the public could not have cared less about Modernist doctrine must have been frustrating for domestic architects of the past three-quarters of a century. So many in search of the American dream were willing to have it interpreted by Colonial Williamsburg, Sears, or a shelter magazine, but not by a European-trained professor.

Modernism as a pure style and idea did not survive the Vietnam War, although a new incarnation of Modern continues, but lacking its original zealotry. Post-Modern, Post-Post-Modern, Deconstructivism, and the current state of American design, show a renewed interest in decoration, as well as a desire not to be limited by a certain philosophy. But all styles reflect someone's worldview as well as their taste, and the best Modern buildings speak of an often bold generation that fervently believed in good design.

AMERICAN DECO

Think of a house with a flat roof, white walls, glass bricks, and some strong horizontal lines reminiscent of a snazzy locomotive. Inside, the bathrooms have black glass on the walls, and the fireplace andirons feature stylized phoenixes, while the tea service is aluminum and shouts of "industrial design." To complete the picture, park a streamlined Chrysler Airflow automobile in the driveway. Although such new Deco houses were found in the same suburban neighborhoods of New York and Los Angeles, the neighbors in their Stockbroker's Tudor and Spanish Mission regarded them as European intruders.

Is there a big difference between what we have come to call Art Deco and the International Style espoused by European Modernists of the same time? In other words, was Deco just Modernism with ornament? To some, Deco is seen as naive Americans' reactions to the machine age or an attempt to humanize the new unornamented style coming from the Bauhaus and other European centers of art and design. Americans typically have fun with their architecture and do not worry about the lineage or their stylistic choices; American Deco, too, has a lot of intriguing non-Euro sources, from Native American, Pre-Columbian, and Frank Lloyd Wright.

American Deco's origins go back to 1925, to an exhibition held that year in Paris called L'Exposition Internationale des Arts Décoratífs et Industriels Modernes (hence both the terms Art Deco and Moderne, although they did not come into common usage until the 1960s). Modernists remember the show for Le Corbusier's iconic Pavilion of the New Spirit. But most of the exhibits were lavish with rich, nonhistorical decoration—a sort of Art Nouveau meets Cubism and the machine. But in the United States, Art Deco was the physical manifestation of the Jazz Age—flashy, devil-may-care, flapper style—and Americans loved it.

Art Deco, or Moderne (as its stripped down and streamlined later version is called), was associated mostly with large public buildings—skyscrapers, bus stations, movie theatres, and power dams. New York's Chrysler Building and Radio City Music Hall are key monuments of the style. In its domestic variations, Deco did not sweep the country like the more popular period styles, but it did have a good run, and it had a lot of influence on interior and industrial design. The flat roofs and streamlined details seemed to offer an element of élan in otherwise discouraging Depression times (even Wright's Fallingwater makes a respectful nod to Art Deco in its use of strong horizontal lines that break in a curve).

The world's fair that should be associated with Deco houses was held in New York in 1939. While the huge pavilions by major corporations such as General Motors and General Electric used streamlined forms, it was the emphasis on the future that gave the style an extra boost on the domestic front. The model homes from the exhibit "Town of Tomorrow," each complete with the latest in appliances and building materials, were built across the country by visitors returning from the fair.

Deco homes were not exactly regional, but the style did lend itself to warmer climates, and so Florida and California were hotbeds of zippy futuristic homes. Deco houses could be built reasonably cheap in concrete, and soon the white stucco was changed to pastels and Deco took on a Caribbean character. Most of all, American Deco houses gave their dwellers a sense of reflected Hollywood glamour—film was the great art form of the 1930s and, like Deco itself, an escapist fantasy during hard times.

HOWARD HOUSE, 1939, San Francisco, California. Henry T. Howard, Architect.

TOP: **HOUSE, ca. 1940**, Wilmette, Illinois. R. W. Scott, Architect. Cubic masses enlivened by a variety of window shapes and whimsical two-disk entrance porch. / BOTTOM: **WESLEY HOUSE, 1937**, Dallas, Texas.

HOUSE, ca. 1936, Tucson, Arizona. Henry Jaastad, Architect. Classically framed symmetrical house with wonderful rhythm of all vertical lines. / **DRAWING: DOLORES DEL RIO HOUSE, 1931**, Santa Monica, California. Front doorway detail. Cedric Gibbons, Designer.

HOUSE, **1934**, Miami Beach, Florida. Robert Law Weed, Architect. / **DRAWING: HOUSE**, **1937**, Albuquerque, New Mexico. Depiction of massing.

TOP: **SHEPPARD HOUSE**, **1934**, San Marino, California. Jock Peters, Architect. / **BOTTOM: SMITH HOUSE**, **1929**, Los Angeles, California. J. C. Smale, Architect. Abstracted, Mayan-like decoration forms an elaborate cornice and parapet.

GENERAL PROPORTIONS

Low, boxy, horizontal.

ROOF TYPES AND FEATURES

Flat roofs hidden behind low parapets.

FENESTRATION

Windows that are combinations of large single panes, with rows of smaller panes to one side. Picture windows. Windows often placed at the corners. Symmetry is a rarity. Glass blocks admit light. If windows have frames, they are decorated with abstract motifs.

STRUCTURAL AND FACEWORK MATERIALS

Stucco walls predominate. Incised horizontal lines, as well as occasional balustrades (particularly on upper story balconies), emphasize the horizontality. Cornices and window surrounds and doorways receive the bulk of the decorative treatment, which is generally comprised of abstract geometrical motifs. Glass bricks can be used as a wall surface and, sometimes, decorative tiles.

SPATIAL DESIGNATION AND FLOOR PLAN

Rectangular, but generally asymmetrical. Flowing, open plan; living and dining and library spaces separated by a step or a low railing.

CHIMNEY PLACEMENT

Pretty much invisible from the street.

ENTRANCEWAY

Doorways can be industrially plain or surrounded by abstract geometric patterns. Doorways often have small, flat roofs above.

COLOR

White, white, white, and sometimes pastel pinks and blues.

HOUSE, **1939**, St. Paul, Minnesota. Curved walls, glass block arranged in a stepped pattern, and porthole windows.

INTERNATIONAL STYLE

In 1932, the Museum of Modern Art held an exhibition called "The International Style: Architecture Since 1922." Codirected by American architect (then the director of the museum's department of architecture) Philip Johnson (b. 1906) and architectural historian Henry-Russell Hitchcock (1903–1987), the exhibition introduced the work of their favorite European Modernists to America (although the show included some Americans, such as Frank Lloyd Wright, George Howe, and Raymond Hood). "International" expressed the style's universality, rather than its geographical range. The exhibit traveled around the United States, the catalogue was published as a book, and given the tastemaker role of the museum, the International Style became a force to be reckoned with in America.

Not since the Richardsonian and Wright's Prairie Style was a style so identified with a few individual architects, in this case the three leaders of the Modern avant-garde in Europe: Germans Walter Gropius (1883–1969) and Ludwig Mies van der Rohe (1886–1969), and Le Corbusier (1887–1965) of Switzerland. Since the 1920s, they had been reshaping the spatial revolution started by Wright. Along with Dutch de Stijl architects such as Gerrit Rietveld (1888–1964) and J. J. P. Oud (1890–1963), the Europeans had created new houses that went even further than Wright in breaking up the box and dissolving traditional domestic boundaries. The spatial planning of Wright was translated into the language of the machine (Le Corbusier even called his paradigm house "A Machine for Living"): flat roofs, factory sash, *pilotis* (cylindrical concrete pillars that raise the structure above ground), glass bricks, and ramps, as well as roof gardens; only a few splashes of primary color offset the purists' white walls. In contrast to the playful Deco, International Style reflected the serious ideological beliefs of its creators.

The heart and soul of the International Style was the Bauhaus, a radical art school in Germany that aspired to the Arts and Crafts ideal of handicraft working in concert with the machine. The Bauhaus attracted most of the avant-garde Modern artists and thinkers in Europe during the 1920s and 1930s, including Paul Klee, Oskar Kokoschka, Josef Albers, and Piet Mondrian. Gropius was the director, as was later Mies. The influence of the Bauhaus grew when the Nazis closed it because many of its teachers and students fled, ultimately ending up in the United States, teaching and practicing here. Gropius taught architecture at Harvard and became a major influence on American architecture. Mies taught and worked in Chicago changing the face of our cities with elegant glass boxes; his glass temple for Dr. Edith Farnsworth, the Farnsworth House (1946–52) in Plano, Illinois, was one of the most controversial homes of the age.

These émigrés collectively created a remarkable statement, setting the course of Modernist design for many years. Walter Gropius's own house (see page 359) in Lincoln, Massachusetts, is one of the classics of the style, with its open plan, flat roof, and factory windows, while his Bauhaus student and Harvard colleague Marcel Breuer built next door. Richard Neutra, a Viennese immigrant, created in 1929 the classic International Style house for Dr. Philip Lovell, the Lovell Health House, in Los Angeles. Philip Johnson's own glass home in New Canaan, Connecticut, done as a tribute to Mies, became an instant—some would say, infamous—landmark. Johnson's homage to the movement was misunderstood by the general public and not much emulated.

Builders or buyers never embraced the International Style, although certain Modernist ideas and details trickled down after World War II. Most of the houses of this style are thus usually associated with the new Europeans and their immediate followers. There were those who felt the International Style was somehow un-American. In his masterpiece Fallingwater, Wright acknowledged the younger Europeans, although in using flat roofs, metal sash, and great sweeping cantilevers, he was no doubt showing them how the style should really be done.

ENTENZA HOUSE, **1937**, Pacific Palisades, California. H. H. Harris, Architect. Flat roofs, factory sash, and exterior staircase could pass for a Dutch or German house of the 1920s, yet this is a work by one of California's leading Modernists. Restored in 1998 by Michael Folonis, Architect. / **DRAWING: MANDEL HOUSE**, **1933–34**, Bedford Hills, New York. Depiction of massing and fenestration. Edward Durell Stone, Architect.

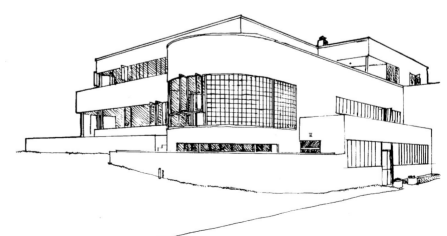

TOP: HOUSE, 1937, Houston, Texas. Wirtz and Calhoun, Architects. Flat roofs, composition of intersecting cubes, and an abstract pattern created by the almost industrial windows. Restored in 2001 by Glassman, Shoemake & Maldonado, Architects. / **BOTTOM: HOUCK HOUSE, 1947**, Houston, Texas. Harry G. Grogan, Architect. Although the house sports the circular walls common to Deco, there is no decoration here at all.

OPPOSITE: DOUBLE HOUSE, **1937**, San Francisco, California. Richard Neutra and Otto Winkler, Architects. Viennese immigrant Neutra brought a pure European Modernism to California. / **TOP: HOUSE**, **1937**, Houston, Texas. Campbell and Keller, Architects. Note how large windows bite into the corners, thus dematerializing the corner. / **BOTTOM: HOUSE**, **1937**, Houston, Texas. Harvin Moore and Herman Lloyd, Architects.

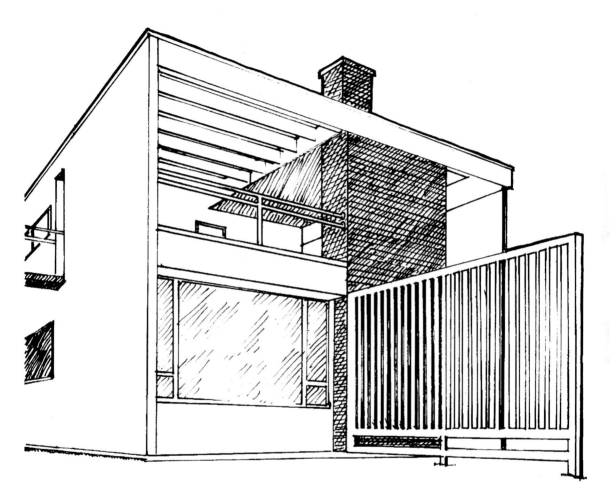

OPPOSITE, TOP: **PERKINS HOUSE**, **1955**, Pasadena, California. Richard Neutra, Architect. Taking some of Wright's ideas a step farther, Neutra's roof seems to float free of the house. / BOTTOM: **GROKOWSKY HOUSE**, **1928**, Pasadena, California. R. M. Schindler, Architect. Another Viennese architect whose decoration-free houses fit right into the Southern California climate and lifestyle. / **GROPIUS HOUSE**, **CA. 1937**, Lincoln, Massachusetts. Rear facade detail. Walter Gropius and Marcel Breuer, Architects.

OPPOSITE, TOP: ROSS HOUSE, **1938**, Los Angeles, California. Raphael Soriano, Architect. / **MIDDLE: BUCK HOUSE**, **1934**, Los Angeles, California. R. M. Schindler, Architect. / **BOTTOM: BEARD HOUSE**, **1934**, Altadena, California. Richard Neutra, Architect. / **GROPIUS HOUSE**, **1937–38**, Lincoln, Massachusetts. Walter Gropius and Marcel Breuer, Architects. The former Bauhaus director and Harvard professor's physical demonstration of the International Style: factory, sash, flat roof, glass bricks, and sculptural spiral staircase (yet with vertical clapboarding, a tribute to New England houses); inexpensive materials, but with elegant results.

international style notes on the defining characteristics

GENERAL PROPORTIONS

Asymmetrical, horizontal massing composed of rectangular cubes: mostly right angles, with occasional semi-circular walls. Usually one or two stories.

SPATIAL DESIGNATION AND FLOOR PLAN

Cubic blocks arranged in L-shapes. Intersecting blocks, with wings often cantilevered. Main living spaces are open, although a step, column, or railing may define areas.

ROOF TYPES AND FEATURES

Flat roofs, sometimes used as sun decks (exterior stairways and pipe railings). Balconies have nautically-inspired pipe railings.

CHIMNEY PLACEMENT

Chimneys are sometimes an important focal point of "radiating" plan and can be fairly massive (although never square). Chimneys can be quite industrial: undisguised metal stacks.

FENESTRATION

Ribbon or strip windows of factory sash, with single panes, invariably vertical. Windows are set right against the facade. Sometimes round, portholelike windows.

ENTRANCEWAY

Industrial-looking doors, never set on axis, and often placed unceremoniously to the side or rear.

STRUCTURAL AND FACEWORK MATERIALS

Examples may have steel frames, but exterior surfaces are usually smooth stucco, although clapboards (vertical as well as horizontal), metal, and concrete are employed as well. Any decoration is eschewed.

COLOR

White, off-white, and the colors inherent in materials used for cladding.

JOSEPH GODDEYNE HOUSE, 1939, Bay City, Michigan. Front facade detail.

MODERN

Modern houses became mainstream following World War II. The bold experiments of the European émigrés before the war were emulated by architects trained by Bauhaus masters, and also by developers looking for something "new." Civilization had been saved—not least through technology—and new materials such as aluminum and plastic were thought to hold the key to creating new housing for everyone.

The 1950s were a time of boundless optimism: kitchens would be all-electric, and all sorts of time-saving appliances would create abundant leisure for the modern family. Cars—always an important indicator in American culture—sported dramatic, aerodynamic tailfins, acres of chromium-trimmed sheet metal, and engines as powerful as bombers. Air-conditioning, along with new kinds of glazing, insulation, and various wonder materials, made it possible to build flat-roofed, often cellarless houses that hugged the ground; superfluous ornament had gone the way of wartime gasoline rationing. The leader of the Free World seemingly neutralized fears of nuclear war by playing a lot of golf, there was meat in the Frigidaire, and life was good.

There was, however, a strong conservative streak in much new home design of the postwar years. The huge new housing developments for returning veterans, like Levittown, featured a standard, replicated house with a gable roof that was a contemporary version of the time-honored Cape Cod cottage. Add shutters, a picket fence, and voilà!—a vision of an America from securer, less angst-ridden times. On the other hand, the popular Ranch House of the period was the direct descendant of Frank Lloyd Wright's Prairie and Usonian designs. (America accepted Wright's housing visions, but not Le Corbusier's.)

But in terms of architect-designed houses, the way had been prepared by the International Style, so the postwar Modern period was one of experimentation, dynamism, excitement, and some real strides in integrating Modernist ideas into an American aesthetic. There was lots of glass, lots of open plans, and some inventive-if-somewhat-crazy schemes, like Tech Built's prefabricated steel house. But Modern architects still thought in terms of a housing revolution, especially through kit houses and mass manufacturing. As we have seen so often in the past, American house designers surpassed their European mentors. The ever-inventive Charles and Ray Eames's own house in Pacific Palisades, California, at first glance looks not unlike a Modernist masterpiece in Holland or Brazil, yet the house is constructed entirely of materials ordered from stock building catalogues.

Despite the universality of Modernism (a house on Long Island or in suburban Minneapolis could look a lot alike), we developed some strong regional expressions, like the Florida beach houses of Paul Rudolph and the reinterpretation of the vernacular California house by a group of architects working in Berkeley. The primacy of Ivy League/International Style architectural education was challenged by state schools in places such as Raleigh and Seattle, Austin and Los Angeles.

By the 1970s, the low-slung cubes with flat roofs, glass walls, and living rooms filled with butterfly chairs, Isamu Noguchi tables, and George Nelson lamps, were beginning to look dated. Who would have thought that these houses would have become period? A great Modern house can hold its own against the best of other styles. But a lot of the things that were inspired by worship of the machine—prefabrication, ease of construction, and inexpensive materials—were copied by developers who neither understood the aesthetic nor the rationale. So a flat roof or an unadorned wall was simply cheaper to build, and then sold by trading in on the cachet of Modernism. As a result, many Modern houses were poorly constructed, and many are showing their age. Rather than inspiring yet another generation of the same, there was a reaction to the Brave New World of Modern architecture: Americans, always slightly uncomfortable with the avant-garde, wanted houses that looked more like what they thought houses ought to look like.

TOP: **ESHERICK HOUSE**, **1959–61**, Philadelphia, Pennsylvania. Louis Kahn, Architect. Kahn's approach to Modernism was a mix of Beaux-Arts training and a personal exploration of basic form. / **BOTTOM: HOUSE**, **1938**, San Francisco, California. John E. Dinwiddie, Architect. / **OPPOSITE: EAMES HOUSE**, **1948**, Pacific Palisades, California. Charles Eames, Architect. The ever-inventive and witty Charles and Ray Eames built this house entirely of stock items from building catalogues.

OPPOSITE: **EGAN HOUSE**, **1957**, Seattle, Washington. Robert Reichert, Architect. / **TOP: TURZAK HOUSE**, **1938–9**, Chicago, Illinois. Bruce Goff, Architect. / **BOTTOM: THAXTON HOUSE**, **1954**, Houston, Texas. Frank Lloyd Wright, Architect.

TOP: HODGSON HOUSE, **1950–51**, New Canaan, Connecticut. Philip Johnson, Architect. /
MIDDLE: HOUSE, **1957**, New Canaan, Connecticut. Sherwood, Mills & Smith, Architects. /
BOTTOM: NOYES HOUSE, **1957**, New Canaan, Connecticut. Eliot Noyes, Architect.

TOP: **HOUSE, ca. 1952**, Palm Springs, California. A desert house featuring a butterfly roof. / BOTTOM: **HOUSE, 1962**, New Canaan, Connecticut. Hugh Smallen, Architect. / **PAGES 368–369: SENSING HOUSE, 1955**, Phoenix, Arizona. Allied Builders, Builder. Ranch House Style.

OPPOSITE, TOP: **HOUSE**, **ca. 1964**, Houston, Texas. Contemporary Style. / **MIDDLE: HOUSE**, **1973**, Galveston, Texas.
Joseph F. Cooley, Architect. Contemporary Style. / **BOTTOM: HOUSE**, **ca. 1961**, Houston, Texas. Contemporary Style. /
GROSS HOUSE, **1957**, Phoenix, Arizona. Allied Builders, Builder. Contemporary Style.

GENERAL PROPORTIONS

Classic Modern houses are one story, spread out, and decidedly horizontal.

ROOF TYPES AND FEATURES

Flat, or sometimes slight single pitch, and more rarely, slight double-pitched gable, often asymmetrical.

FENESTRATION

Floor-to-ceiling glass in living sections, horizontal strips in less public parts of the house. Glazing can reach up to the eaves. Ranch House examples may have horizontal strips of windows.

STRUCTURAL AND FACEWORK MATERIALS

Modern examples have greater variety of wall coverings than International Style, and balloon framing is more common than a steel skeleton; some stone and brick, but mostly flush-sided vertical clapboarding; Ranch House examples have horizontal siding. The only thing approaching decoration would be a larger chimney made of brick or stone. Late Modern examples may use more natural materials, especially wood such as redwood or cedar.

SPATIAL DESIGNATION AND FLOOR PLAN

Very open plans, usually with kitchen, dining area, and living room being one continuous space; bedrooms are often off to one side—spread out from the main living area. Carports are a hallmark of the style; their roofs are extensions of the main horizontal lines. Even if a masonry or stone base, examples seem to sit on the ground, and many sit on concrete slabs. Basements, and especially attics, are rare.

CHIMNEY PLACEMENT

Often appear at the peak of a double-pitched roof and can be substantial and made of stone. More Wright (especially in Ranch House versions) than International Style in inspiration.

ENTRANCEWAY

Common is a somewhat formal main entrance, but decoration is limited, for example, to a floor-to-ceiling glass sidelight. Entry is generally from the carport into the kitchen or utility room.

COLOR

White predominates, although the machine aesthetic of the International Style is augmented by warmer paint colors. Later examples, particularly on the West Coast, favor natural colors.

TOWERS HOUSE, 1956–58, Essex, Connecticut. Front-entry facade detail. Ulrich Franzen, Architect.

13

POST-MODERN REFERS TO THE ARCHITECTURE AFTER MODERNISM. If not downright specific, Post-Modern does have a certain direct utility. (Eventually, all of the newer styles may be combined with other styles, given new names, or discontinued.) It has come to mean modern buildings using elements of past styles in new, often humorous ways.

Modernism was never the monolith that its proponents claimed. There were signs as early as the 1960s that Americans were just not happy with Modern houses, whether Ranch or International Style. A case for Wright's open plan can be made, but we missed the good old double-pile plan. We wanted a central hall and rooms arrayed in a logical pattern, and even doorways and doors. Most of all, we yearned for houses that looked like us and that spoke to us of our past. Architectural theory be damned, we wanted Cape Cod cottages, we wanted to feel all right about liking Colonial and Georgian, and we knew it is human nature to want ornament on our dwellings.

If everyday folks were disenchanted with Modernity, much of the academy was still in the hands of the International Style crowd. The greatest challenge to the hegemony of Modernism was the historic preservation movement. Americans were discovering their physical history, and they were getting fed up with seeing it torn down. While professors wearing the kind of round eyeglasses that had become Le Corbusier's trademark were preaching that houses be on stilts, and have ramps and factory-made windows, we were visiting Colonial Williamsburg, Virginia, and Old Sturbridge Village, Massachusetts, as well as a Europe where historic preservation was often an instrument of national policy. As tourists we sought out villages with cobbled streets lined with old cottages.

Then a revolutionary manifesto appeared in 1966: a book called *Complexity and Contradiction in Architecture*, published by the Museum of Modern Art, publishers of *The International Style* thirty-four years before. Author Robert Venturi (b. 1925) argued that ornament was not a sin but a normal aspect of architecture. Furthermore, the Princeton-trained polemicist called for study of the past as basic inspiration for designing the future. *Complexity* emboldened architects to break from the orthodoxy of Miesian Modernism.

Venturi's modest buildings changed the domestic landscape. The house that he designed for his mother near Philadelphia (see page 380) became Post-Modernism's first landmark. The inexpensively constructed house was shaped like a classical pediment; it has a Roman bath window of the kind used by Palladio and a simple belt course—a classical device for dividing a building and maintaining proportions. Venturi's mother's house shocked because it was clearly a suburban box, but with an overlay of architectural history. Venturi's allusions to the past were often playful and ironic.

Similar wry jokes popped up in houses by other Post-Modernists. Charles Moore (1925–1993, also Princeton-trained) employed out-of-scale but recognizable columns and other references to the Renaissance. Robert A. M. Stern (b. 1939) evolved from designing houses with Venturi-like classical details to a mature interpretation of some of America's better home styles, particularly the Shingle Style. Other architects, especially on the West Coast, discovered vernacular farmhouses and, along with Moore, created a "shed-roof" style with affinities to utilitarian barns and humbler outbuildings.

The interest in the past, ironically, also fostered a revival of early Modernism. Architects such as Michael Graves (b. 1934), Charles Gwathmey (b. 1938), and Richard Meier (b. 1934), built houses that mimicked Le Corbusier's early houses, complete with curved ramps, *pilotis*, glass blocks, sunscreens, and open roofs. Peter Eisenman's Roman Numeral–named houses were even more theoretical than their Dutch de Stijl sources. Yet these were creative, not slavish imitations of earlier work, and they opened the way for freer interpretations of the past. Graves, for example, abandoned the 1920s white-on-white palette in favor of rich pastels, along with an enlarged vocabulary of classical forms.

So, what seemed at first a unified response to Modernism, turned out to be much more complex and contradictory. (The New Urbanism movement with its quaint new villages and neo-Georgian styles is one legacy of Post-Modernism.) Post-Modernism however, offered Americans a variety of rich domestic expression.

VENTURI HOUSE, **1962**, Chestnut Hill, Pennsylvania. Venturi and Rauch, Architects. This revolutionary house is composed like a giant pediment; almost every element is an historical reference. / **OPPOSITE, TOP: LANG HOUSE**, **1973–74**, Washington, Connecticut. Robert A. M. Stern, Architect. / **BOTTOM: PHILLIPS STUDIO AND HOUSE**, **1977**, Houston, Texas. W. Irving Phillips, Jr., Architect.

post-modern notes on the defining characteristics

GENERAL PROPORTIONS

The range of the Post-Modern house is varied, but it often almost looks like a period house with exaggerated elements.

ROOF TYPES AND FEATURES

Any of a variety of roofs is possible, although the neo-Corbusians employ flat roofs, while the single-pitch shed roof is a characteristic of the "inclusivist" camp of Post-Modernism.

FENESTRATION

Many of the traditional windows are resurrected from the past, from double-hung sash to Palladian bath windows or even windows recycled from factories. Often placed seemingly at random, windows can act as signifiers of the house's stylistic ancestry.

STRUCTURAL AND FACEWORK MATERIALS

Post-Modern houses are built of a variety of materials: barn siding, shingles, clapboards, stucco, decorative tiles. Details can include super graphics, columns, International Style pilotis, and other references to the past—often applied in whimsical, non-sensical, apparently irrational ways.

SPATIAL DESIGNATION AND FLOOR PLAN

Generalizations are difficult with Post-Modern, yet a majority of the houses have rather traditional box-like plans.

CHIMNEY PLACEMENT

All sorts of chimneys are used, from massive brick ones to basic metal pipes.

ENTRANCEWAY

Doorways can be so modest as to be unobtrusive or they can be playful recreations of past styles, complete with columns, entablatures, or porches, but with proportions noticeably—sometimes perversely—different from their sources.

COLOR

Natural-wood, plus white, pastels, and bright color accents.

ROSS-LACY HOUSE, **1993**, Sherman, Connecticut. Gable and fenestration detail. Centerbrook Architects.

deconstructivism

deconstructivism

LIKE KIDS RELEASED FROM SCHOOL THE LAST DAY BEFORE SUMMER, American architecture sprinted off in several directions following Post-Modernism. Modernism had been overthrown (or at least revealed to be but another in the march of historical styles), but Post-Modernism did not seem to have staying power beyond its liberating call for experimentation.

The East Coast's architectural hegemony had also been overthrown. New York still might have been the center of the art world, but architectural leadership, like almost everything else in American culture, had moved south and west: Los Angeles was the new design center. Just as Venturi's house for his mother was a landmark for Post-Modernism, Frank Gehry's Santa Monica house (1978–79; see page 397) announced more radical change. Gehry (b. 1929) transformed a nondescript Dutch Colonial suburban house by cutting a new addition through the old house at unusual and somewhat disturbing angles; he also wrapped part of the house in chain-link fencing and corrugated metal sheets. The witty and ironic Canadian-born architect, who was first noticed for his strong and curvaceous cardboard furniture, pointed out that fish had been around a lot longer than Greek columns and iconically used fish motifs for both buildings and furniture. (Gehry's ichthyology morphed into unprecedented ribbonlike forms for such monuments as the titanium-wrapped Guggenheim Museum in Bilbao, Spain.)

Gehry was only one of a group of cerebral, edgy West Coast designers.

The late Franklin Israel (1945–1996), a former Hollywood set designer, created dramatically surprising houses with strong diagonal structural elements, bright colors, a variety of materials, and a respectful nod to California's vernacular landscape. Morphosis, the Santa Monica-based firm of American architect Thomas Mayne (b. 1943), does similar fiddling with the odd juxtapositions of clashing elements, while mixing materials, colors, and stylistic sources. The result is a controlled, elegant violence. The houses of architect Eric Owen Moss (b. 1943) are also beautifully constructed, but what one feels is the exploded geometry (memories of Le Corbusier's early houses) and restless, clashing connections. A Moss house often looks as though a bite had been taken out of it by some concrete-eating ogre; through the missing bits one ambiguously glimpses more of the house.

This Los Angeles style has plenty of adherents elsewhere. Ecuadorian Carlos Zapata (b. 1961), working in Florida, is equally adept at deconstructing his houses and putting them back together again, but with a lighter touch. Michael Rotondi (b. 1949), one of the founders of Morphosis, works on both coasts. His construction details are carefully executed; the angled shapes clash a little more gently, while the fenestration appears intuitive. Yale professor Turner Brooks has been building inexpensive deconstructed frame houses in Vermont.

Recalling that Austrian architects Rudolph Schindler and Richard Neutra created revolutionary houses in Los Angeles early in the last century, Coop Himmelb(l)au's 3er House in Venice Beach (see page 391) continues the tradition.

DRAWING: BLADES HOUSE, **1995**, Santa Barbara, California. Front facade detail. Morphosis Architects. / **FRANK W. HULES IV HOUSE**, **1986**, Atlanta, Georgia. Anthony Ames, Architect. / **OPPOSITE: 3 ER HOUSE**, **2002**, Venice, California. Coop Himmelb(l)au, Architects.

HOUSE, **1979–82**, Pacific Palisades, California. Eric Owen Moss, Architect.

2-4-6-8 HOUSE, **1979**, Venice, California. Mayne and Rotundi, Architects. Window is deconstructed and becomes like a billboard; nothing is quite what it seems, except the inexpensive materials. House teases, stretches credulity.

, **1989**, Venice, California. Brian Murphy, Architect.

GEHRY HOUSE, **1978**, Santa Monica, California. Frank Gehry, Architect. An everyday house and everyday materials (plywood, chain link fencing, corrugated metal) made over and put together at odd angles and in unexpected ways.

OPPOSITE: HOUSE, 2004, Santa Monica, California. / **NORTON HOUSE**, **1983–84**, Venice, California. Frank Gehry, Architect. Logs, guy wires, different colors, and a studio/retreat space on a single column; ingenious solution to narrow lot.

deconstructivism notes on the defining characteristics

GENERAL PROPORTIONS

Deconstructivist houses defy proportional canons. Sense of multiple—clashing or oddly interlocking—forms predominates.

ROOF TYPES AND FEATURES

Lead-coated copper is used a lot, as are gently arched roofs (composed of a small segment of an enormous circle). Roofs can be flat, rounded, diagonal, multi-sloped, and several types may be employed on one house.

FENESTRATION

Can have many window types: curved, mullionless, trapezoidal, even windows set within windows, and may be placed almost anywhere.

STRUCTURAL AND FACEWORK MATERIALS

Examples benefit from steel frames and reinforced concrete, although a wide range and great variety of materials are employed: concrete (preferably cast and smooth), copper and zinc (treated with different coatings), wood, stucco, wrought iron, and even traditional materials like concrete blocks, marble, and onyx.

SPATIAL DESIGNATION AND FLOOR PLAN

Spaces may rise two or three stories and interact with intruding horizontal spaces at any point along the way. An open space may be dissected by a structural column. There are no rules, except for breaking them.

CHIMNEY PLACEMENT

Chimneys can be sculptural, decorative, or utilitarian.

ENTRANCEWAY

Doors may be the most "normal" feature of the Deconstructivist house, although they may be located in unusual places, such as directly on a corner, and composed of a surprising combination of materials.

COLOR

Many and varied colors, primarily provided by the materials employed, although bright tiles and pastel stucco finishes are used.

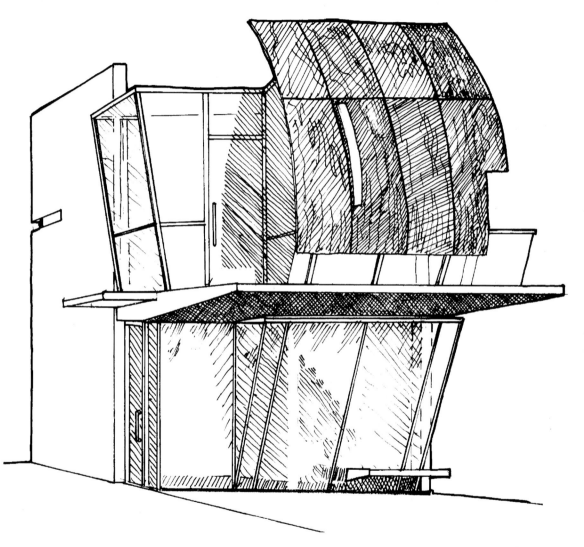

LANDES GUEST HOUSE, **1994**, Golden Beach, Florida. Front facade detail. Carlos Zapata, Architect.

AMERICAN HOUSE STYLES, LIKE AMERICAN CULTURE IN GENERAL, have had their fair share of curiosities. Some of these were styles that failed to achieve popularity, or went out of fashion quickly, or involved forms and materials that were too far ahead of their times. Yet, there are many of these intriguing footnotes—expressions of experimental genius or just plain quirkiness.

The Egyptian Revival simply did not lend itself to houses, although a few examples exist. While ancient Egypt excited the nineteenth-century Romantic, the heavy style was better suited to prisons and funerary monuments than houses. Moorish, too, survives in a few houses, but mostly in details, like the characteristic Islamic horse-shoe-shaped arches. The exoticism of the world of the Alhambra may have been in the mind of builders of the huge octagonal house in Natchez, Mississippi, known as Nutt's Folly (1860), not to mention P. T. Barnum's house, Iranistan (1849), in Bridgeport, Connecticut.

The octagon itself was a short-lived though very lively phenomenon. There are probably a hundred surviving houses from the Octagon Mode's heyday during the dozen years before the Civil War. Phrenologist Orson Squire Fowler advocated happy and healthful living through building eight-sided houses. Octagons were built in masonry, brick, and frame (Fowler recommended a kind of concrete), often with elaborate cupolas (which facilitated air circulation) and with a variety of stylistic treatments (usually Greek, Gothic, or Italianate). The benefits—real or purported—of octagonal living did not outweigh people's natural propensity for rectangular rooms.

Round houses were advocated by another cosmic thinker and builder, Buckminster Fuller. His Dymaxion House of 1929 was a prototype for a prefabricated metal house constructed on a central mast (so it could rotate to follow the sun or to change views). The bathrooms, kitchens, and even the car that Fuller designed for the house's occupants owed more to contemporary automotive manufacturing and aeronautical engineering than age-old carpentry and masonry. Fuller's ideas were both revolutionary and practical; nevertheless most Americans found the ideas too futuristic, and they did not want to live in round metal homes.

Prefabrication has a long history in American houses. It certainly seemed the wave of the future following World War II. Inventor Carl Stradlund wanted to do for American housing what General Motors had done for the car. His all-steel house came off an assembly line, was trucked to the site and assembled in a few days, using only screwdrivers and wrenches. The Lustron House was made completely of porcelain-enameled steel and was touted as virtually maintenance-free. Two-thousand-five-hundred houses were built over five years, and although various theories may explain Lustron's collapse, much of the reason was style—or perceived lack of it. The Cape Cod or Levittown was the ticket.

There are always architects who wish to change the domestic landscape. Bruce Goff, a student of Wright's, and Bart Prince, a follower of Goff's, attempted expressionistic houses (see page 410) that are anthropomorphic—like giant centipedes. Another individual approach that hooks into our love of the automobile was Daniel V. Scully's *Carchitecture*. Scully's own house in Dublin, New Hampshire, combines regional Greek Revival and Shingle Style elements, although the house is in the shape of an old Pontiac; license plates serve as metopes, while a dragster body holds the wood stove.

And while ever interesting, such curiosities must be a nightmare for the real estate salesperson. Which is not to say that we are totally conformist, for we individualize the most cookie cutter of houses. But tradition keeps reappearing in the American house—just like the child's drawing of the house, with a triangular gable end, a smoking chimney, and a multilight window.

BUBBLE HOUSE, 1946, Pasadena, California. Wallace Neff, Architect. Like some sort of primitive hut or perhaps a Hopi Hogan or a Mongolian yurt. / DRAWING: THE DYMAXION MOUSE, 1944–45, Wichita, Kansas. R. Buckminster Fuller, Architect.

HOUSE, ca. 1989, Marina del Rey, California.

DRAWING: **GLEBE HOUSE**, **ca. 1850**, Arlington, Virginia. Front elevation. / **OCTAGON**, **ca. 1860**, Providence, Rhode Island.

FEUSIER OCTAGON, **1857**, San Francisco, California. This eight-sided home has Italianate details (quoins and cornice brackets), but a variety of mid-nineteenth-century styles were employed to embellish octagon houses.

HOUSE, **1960**, Houston, Texas. Bruce Goff with Joseph Krakower, Architects. /
DRAWING: PRINCE HOUSE, **1985**, Albuquerque, New Mexico. Front elevation.
Bart Prince, Architect.

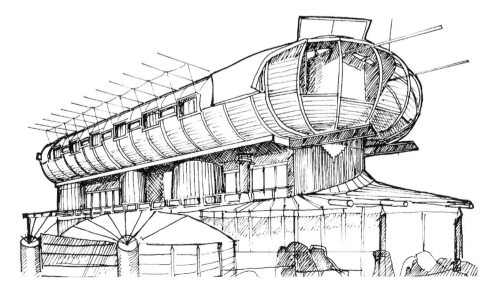

ROUTE 101 TWO-LANE HIGHWAY HOME, **1981**, Dublin, New Hampshire. Daniel V. Scully, Architect. With respectful homage to the region's Greek Revival farmhouses and later Shingle Style summer cottages, Scully's own house also has a kitchen shaped like the hood of a Pontiac, complete with Indian-head weathervane.

LUSTRON HOUSE, ca. 1948, Louisville, Kentucky.

LUSTRON HOUSE, **1948**, Minneapolis, Minnesota.

house styles now

IT MAY BE TOO SOON to talk of the current state of house styles, but perhaps some general comments will be useful. Predictions are both tricky and unreliable, and one generation's high style is dismissed or ignored by another's. Still, the richness and variety of American domestic architecture continues to provide us with much to watch, and a lot to praise. ▪ Good design never goes out of fashion, and some of the older generation of house designers have matured, gathering the best lessons from past styles, particularly Modernism. Their younger protégés— Steven Holl, Mack Scogin and Merrill Elam, and Richard Fernau and Laura Hartman, to name only a few contemporary architects, are building American houses that will influence the next class of domestic designers and that will be the subject of tomorrow's historians. ▪ Regional architecture, despite a wave of homogenization in almost everything else cultural, has become one of the strongest expressions of the American dream, as house designers respond to the desert (Antoine Predock), the rain-forest climate of the Pacific Northwest (James Cutler), the Minnesota Prairie (David Salmela), or Latino Florida (Arquitectonica). Green design, too, while an assumed, unselfconscious way of building for many of our ancestors, is changing the way we design and build houses. ▪ One of the most encouraging architectural developments of our time is the Rural Studio in Alabama, the brainchild of the late Samuel Mockbee (1944–2001). Mockbee and the architectural students from Auburn University who were a part of his design/build workshop have helped some of America's poorest families to build homes, hope, and identity by demonstrating that houses made of recycled materials can provide dignity as well as shelter. ■ Social responsibility is not, unfortunately, part of what may be the most prevalent contemporary house type: the McMansion. The pop-culture name seems appropriate, describing as it does houses that reflect both wealth and a production-line approach to design. Like fast-food stores, these new houses have spread across former farmland along with the ubiquitous shopping malls. New money minted in the boom of the 1990s wanted new houses, but the stylistic emphasis is almost exclusively on the past: Colonial, Georgian, Shingle Style, Victorian, but never Modern. The stylistic-parts bin seems to have been raided without rhyme or reason, as various elements are often mixed in the same building. ■ The McMansion, complete with a three-car garage (never less, often more), designer kitchens, what their developers call "Palladium" windows, two-story grand entrance halls, and a cacophony of roof pitches (at least on the front of the house), lack the careful attention to detail that we admire in Early American homes. The materials are cheap, and despite overinflated prices from Maine to California, these pretentious would-be palatial homes are only a very faint echo of the robber baron spirit. While the houses of every age have had their critics, it is difficult to imagine earlier styles that sit so poorly on the landscape and are so poorly built. ■ *The Abrams Guide to American House Styles* is not intended to facilitate copying from the past, but to offer inspiration for building upon and learning from four centuries of great houses.

MCMANSIONS, ca. 2000, These examples happen to be in New Jersey, Kentucky, and Texas, but they could be anywhere in the country. Drawing upon past styles, both American and European, and sometimes quite attractive, McMansion developments are like Potemkin Villages: all facade, designed to impress.

glossary

ACROTERION / Greek decorative element at peak of gable, or at the outside edge, as decorative detail.

ADAM, ROBERT (1728–1792) / Scottish architect who championed the revival of Roman forms. His neoclassicism, very influential, is often called the Adam Style.

ASHLAR / Smooth-cut (in contrast to rough-cut or rock-faced) blocks of stone used in building.

BALLOON FRAME / Method of house construction using precut lumber to build the structural frame, most typically standard 2"x 4" lumber spaced 16" on center for most vertical elements.

BALUSTRADE / A railing system composed of uprights (called balusters) and a top rail, sometimes also a bottom rail, used on stairways and balconies.

BARGEBOARD / A board covering the end of the roof structure on a gable-ended house.

BATTLEMENT / At the roofline, a fortified parapet with alternate solid sections and openings. Originally a defense design (firearms could be placed in the crenels) common to a fortress, it was later adopted as a decorative motif for use domestically.

BAUHAUS / Revolutionary school of architecture and design that promoted a Modernist aesthetic. It was founded in Germany after World War I. Later, many of its teachers and students moved to the United States, where they had a significant influence on Modernism.

CARPORT / A roofed parking area attached to a house, usually without walls; variant of the earlier

porte cochère. The word was coined by Frank Lloyd Wright.

CARTOUCHE / An ornamental panel used in a building facade; can be round, oval, or shaped like a piece of paper or a scroll.

CASEMENT WINDOW / A type of window hinged on one side.

CHATEAU / Originally meaning a French castle, the word ultimately came to be used to imply a large house or estate—usually one built of masonry with large, steeply pitched roofs, often with towers and turrets.

CLAPBOARD / A wooden piece of horizontal siding, usually thicker at the bottom than the top, installed in an overlapping fashion. Called a *weatherboard* in England.

CORNICE / The projecting, often decorative, molding at the horizontal top edge of a wall or building.

CRENEL / An open space between the merlons of a battlement.

CRESTING / Decorative ironwork at the top edge of a roof or tower.

DE STIJL / Dutch for "The Style." A design movement founded in 1917 by artists and architects Mondrian, van Doesburg, Oud, Rietveld, and others in Holland, De Stijl's adherents subscribed to and promoted the notion of a universal modern style, sometimes called *Elementalism*.

DORMER / A vertical, or upright, window lighting the space under a roof. A dormer projects from the slope of the roof and has a roof of its own.

From the word *dormir*, French for "to sleep", as the space lit was usually used for sleeping.

EAVE / The projecting lower edge of a roof.

ECLECTICISM / The concept of using a variety of historical styles in the design of a new building.

ELIZABETHAN / Style of architecture (mostly domestic) corresponding roughly to the reign of Elizabeth I (1558–1603). Characteristics include large windows and strapwork decoration. It has elements of both Medieval and Renaissance architecture.

ENTABLATURE / The horizontal upper part of a classical facade that is carried by the columns.

FANLIGHT / A window, typically positioned over a front door in Georgian architecture, in the shape of a fan. Windows were commonly called "lights." May be semi-circular or elliptical.

FENESTRATION / The pattern of windows in a building. After the French word for "window," *fenêtre*.

FINIAL / Decorative vertical element forming the top of a gable, spire, tower, etc.

FRET / Geometric ornament of intertwined horizontal and vertical lines, usually in the form of a band.

GABLE / The triangular upper portion of a wall carrying a roof formed by two slanting sides.

GAMBREL / A roof type characterized by a double pitch on each side.

GIBBS, JAMES (1682–1754) / English Baroque architect, his *A Book of Architecture*, 1728, disseminated both his work and that of Palladio; it became a popular reference in both England and America.

GOTHIC / Architectural style of medieval times characterized by the use of the pointed arch, ribbed vault, the flying buttress. It enjoyed a revival in the United States in the early nineteenth century in both religious and residential architecture.

GROPIUS, WALTER (1883–1969) / Modernist German architect and teacher, he founded the Bauhaus. Gropius later moved to America and, in addition to maintaining his own architectural practice, taught at the Harvard architecture school.

HALF-TIMBERING / Building style in which the structural timber frame of a house is expressed in visible timbers in the walls.

HIPPED ROOF / A roof type where all four sides of a rectangular building have a vertical roof element above them. The junction where two adjacent sides meet is the hip.

IN ANTIS / Columns are said to be in antis when they are enclosed in a portico that has pilasters or piers at each side. These are called "antae," and columns inside these are said to be in antis.

JONES, INIGO (1573–1652) / Prominent English classical architect strongly influenced by the Italians Serlio and Palladio. Jones was largely responsible for introducing Renaissance forms to England.

LE CORBUSIER (1887–1965) / Charles-Edouard Jeanneret. Swiss-born French architect, very important as architect, city planner, and author.

LINTEL / The top, horizontal structural element of a rectangular door or window.

MANSARD / A type of roof with two pitches—a steep lower section, often with dormers, and a relatively shallow upper section. All four sides are the same, so it resembles a double-hipped roof.

MEDIEVAL / A period in European history from roughly 500 to 1500.

MIES VAN DER ROHE, LUDWIG (1886–1969) / One of the founding fathers of Modern architecture. The last director of the Bauhaus, he moved to the United States, where he taught at the Illinois Institute of Technology, and in his practice built canonical examples of modern houses and skyscrapers.

MULLION / A vertical divider between panes of glass in a window.

OGEE / A type of arch with a double curvature on each side.

PALAZZO / Italian word meaning *palace*, and usually used with relation to Italian palaces or large and impressive houses.

PALLADIO, ANDREA (1508–1580) / Very important as both architect and author. Studied in Rome before beginning a distinguished career in the area around Venice. His *Four Books of Architecture* (*I quattro libri dell'architettura*) of 1570 was enormously influential.

PALLADIAN WINDOW / A window composed of a central arched window flanked by smaller vertical windows.

PALMETTE / A fan-shaped ornament derived from a palm leaf; used in Greek and Greek Revival-style ornament.

PARAPET / In an exterior wall, the part entirely above the roof.

PILASTER / A column attached to a wall, normally flat, projecting slightly.

PORTE COCHÈRE / A covered entry, wide enough to allow carriages or automobiles to pass through.

PLAN / A two-dimensional representation of a house, seen from above in section, as though the top had been taken off.

QUOIN / A large corner block. Used historically as a reinforcement device for the corners of a building. In American architecture, these are more often imitated for purposes of decoration than actually used structurally. From the French word for "corner," *coin*.

RENAISSANCE / Architectural period beginning in Italy around 1400, it marked a return to classical influences in architecture.

REINFORCED CONCRETE / Concrete is a strong building material, formed by mixing an aggregate—sand or gravel—with cement. It is very strong in compression but weak in tension. Introducing steel reinforcing rods to take up the tensile forces makes the combination (reinforced concrete) both strong and versatile.

SALTBOX / New England gabled-roof house with a low addition on the back. The longer slope of the rear roofline makes it resemble a colonial box used to hold salt.

SASH / A window frame that can slide up and down.

STUCCO / A cementitious building material used as an exterior covering on walls.

TERRA-COTTA / Clay ornament, fired but not glazed.

TETRASTYLE / Having four columns in the front.

THATCH, THATCHING / A roof covering made of bundled reeds or straw.

TRANSOM / A horizontal bar across the top of a door, separating the door from the window above. This window is called a *transom window*.

TUDOR REVIVAL STYLE / Architectural style associated with the Tudor dynasty in England (1485–1558), its features include false half-timbering, elaborate and massive chimneys, and strapwork in the gable ends.

USONIAN / A utopian concept of Frank Lloyd Wright that describes an economical variant of the prairie house, which he hoped would become a national standard. It is described in his 1954 book *The Natural House*.

VOUSSOIR / A wedge-shaped stone or brick used in making an arch.

WATER TABLE / A plain or molded projection in the wall a few feet above the ground.

WREN, SIR CHRISTOPHER (1632–1723) / Perhaps England's greatest architect, also a scientist and mathematician. Designed St. Paul's Cathedral in London; his fifty-one London churches had great influence in the United States.

WRIGHT, FRANK LLOYD (1867–1959) / A key figure in Modern architecture, this American architect developed the Prairie Style. His many books promoted his ideas in both architecture and city planning.

Doubilet, Susan, and Daralice Boles. *American House Now: Contemporary Architectural Directions*. New York: Universe, 1997.

Frampton, Kenneth. *American Masterworks: The Twentieth Century American House*. New York: Rizzoli, 1995.

Gowans, Alan. *Styles and Types of North American Architecture: Social Function and Cultural Expression*. New York: HarperCollins, 1992.

Kidder-Smith, G. E. *Source Book of American Architecture*. New York: Princeton Architectural Press, 1996.

McAlester, Virginia, and Lee McAlester. *A Field Guide to American Houses*. New York: Knopf, 1984.

Morrison, Hugh. *Early American Architecture*. New York: Oxford, 1952.

Pearson, Clifford, ed. *Modern American Houses: Four Decades of Award-Winning Designs in Architectural Record*. New York: Abrams, 1996.

Pierson, Jr., William H. *American Buildings and their Architects: Vol. 1, The Colonial And Neoclassical Styles*. Garden City, N.Y.: Doubleday, 1970.

———. *American Buildings and their Architects: Vol. 2, Technology and the Picturesque*. Garden City, N.Y.: Doubleday, 1978.

Scully, Jr., Vincent J. *The Shingle Style and the Stick Style, Rev. Ed*. New Haven: Yale, 1971.

Sommer, Robin Langley. *The American House*. San Diego: Thunder Bay Press, 2000.

index
Page numbers in *italics* refer to illustrations